ESSENTIAL ENGLISH LEGAL SYSTEM

SECOND EDITION

Cavendish
Publishing
Limited

London • Sydney

Titles in the series:

ESSENTIAL ENGLISH LEGAL SYSTEM

SECOND EDITION

Jan McCormick-Watson,
LLB, LLM, PGCE

Cavendish
Publishing
Limited

London • Sydney

First published in Great Britain 1994 by Cavendish Publishing Limited, The Glass House, Wharton Street, London WC1X 9PX

Telephone: 0171-278 8000   Facsimile: 0171-278 8080

E-mail: info@cavendishpublishing.com

Visit our Home Page on http://www.cavendishpublishing.com

McCormick-Watson, Jan

Essential English legal system – 2nd ed – (Essential law series)

1. Law – England 2. Law – Wales

I Title

349.4'2

ISBN 1 85941 361 7

Printed and bound in Great Britain

Foreword

This book is part of the Cavendish Essential series. The books in the series are designed to provide useful revision aids for the hard-pressed student. They are not, of course, intended to be substitutes for more detailed treatises. Other textbooks in the Cavendish portfolio must supply these gaps.

The Cavendish Essential Series is now in its second edition and is a well established favourite among students.

The team of authors bring a wealth of lecturing and examining experience to the task in hand. Many of us can even recall what it was like to face law examinations!

Professor Nicholas Bourne
General Editor, Essential Series
Swansea Law School
Summer 1997

Contents

1 Sources of law

> **You should be familiar with the following areas:**
>
> * common law and equity: the Judicature Acts 1873–75
> * English and European law
> * the legislative process
> * types of delegated legislation and its disadvantages
> * case law

Common law and equity

Pre-Norman Conquest

Under the Saxons there was not such a thing as English law. Communities were small and isolated because travel was dangerous and difficult. The administration of justice was centred locally, each small community having its own court where customs, according to that part of the country, were applied. There was a court in each Shire, and one in each Hundred (a sub-division of a Shire). These courts were dominated by wealthy local landowners and noblemen. There were a few written laws known as King Alfred's laws.

The Norman Conquest

The Norman Conquest replaced this with a stronger centralised system. The Normans utilised the existing structure of courts, developing it and appointing their own judges. The country was divided into 'circuits', which judges would follow, administering justice. They were called *itinerant justices in eyre*. They each visited a circuit of county towns hearing all the cases that had amounted since their last visit to the county.

The emergence of common law

As the judges became more established in their travelling of circuits, there was a unification of the various local customs. The King created new legal rules and gradually local customs were replaced by rules common to the whole country; this eventually became known as the common law. There were few statutes or written laws and judges would look to similar cases to guide them. Thus we can see the emergence of the doctrine of precedent.

Common law and equity

In order to bring an action in the common law courts a writ had to be issued by the chancellor. These writs were very specific in nature. If there was no writ available to fit your particular action then you would be without redress. The Provisions of Oxford 1258 prevented the chancellor's office from creating new writs which led to a very rigid system. The development and growth of the common law system had not been expected and caused difficulties. Many people complained about the injustices that were inherent in the system. Individuals, disenchanted by the system, made pleas to the King for protection. Because of the increasing number of these pleas the chancellor created his own court, punishing those who put too much reliance on the strict operation of the common law.

The Court of Chancery

The Court of Chancery offered a route which enabled individuals to obtain justice alleviating the harshness of the common law. Equitable maxims were developed, such as, 'equity follows the law'. Equity developed its own set of rules which came into conflict with common law rules. This conflict between the two systems came to a head in the *Earl of Oxford's Case* (1615). Here it was decided that if there was conflict between the two systems, equity would prevail.

The defects of equity: Judicature Acts 1873–75

However, equity eventually became as rigid in form as the common law and it suffered many defects. It became overburdened and very slow. Reform became necessary and this came in the shape of the Judicature Acts 1873–75 which fused the two systems together. Common law and equitable remedies were available in all law courts.

Important events in English constitutional history

DATE	EVENT
890	ALFRED'S LAWS
1066	NORMAN CONQUEST
1086	SEPARATION OF CHURCH AND LAY COURTS: DOMESDAY BOOK
1164	JURIES INSTITUTED IN SOME PROCEEDINGS
1215	MAGNA CARTA
1279	STATUTE OF MORTMAIN
1534	REFORMATION
1535	STATUTE OF USES
1601	JAMES 1 SEVERS LINKS WITH SCOTLAND
1629	CHARLES 1 DISSOLUTION OF PARLIAMENT
1649	CROMWELL'S COMMONWEALTH OF ENGLAND
1660	RESTORATION OF CHARLES II
1662	ACT OF SETTLEMENT
1679	HABEAS CORPUS ACT
1689	BILL OF RIGHTS
1701	ACT OF UNION WITH SCOTLAND
1772	ROYAL MARRIAGE ACT
1832	REFORM ACT
1867	SECOND REFORM ACT
1911	PARLIAMENT ACT LIMITING POWER OF HOUSE OF LORDS
1949	PARLIAMENT ACT
1958	LIFE PEERAGES ACT
1963	PEERAGE ACT
1972	EUROPEAN COMMUNITIES ACT
1986	SINGLE EUROPEAN ACT
1992	TREATY ON EUROPEAN UNION: MAASTRICHT TREATY

English and European law

Institutions of the EEC

The European Parliament
The European Parliament meets in Strasbourg. It has no legislative powers. It is responsible for the community budget and possesses the power to freeze community spending. It has the power to sack the entire Commission if it chooses, but is unable to sack an individual Commissioner. It is a directly elected body of 518 Members of the European Parliament, they are elected for five years. Each Member State is allocated seats in accordance with the population of that State. Various committees are formed, for example, agriculture, fisheries, food, transport, social matters, employment. Proposals from the Commission pass through these committees before being sent to the Councils of Ministers.

The Council of Ministers
The Council of Ministers is based in Brussels and could be said to be the actual legislative body of the Community, because this is where the major decisions are taken. It consists of 12 members, one from each Member State. Voting is by 'qualified majority', the States' votes are weighted, eg UK has 10 votes whereas Spain has eight votes. A qualified majority is achieved by gaining 62 out of the total of 87 votes. Ministers from the Member States meeting together form the Council of Ministers. The Presidency of the Council changes hands between Member States every six months. The Council of Ministers is a series of Councils containing Ministers of each Member State responsible for the specific items under consideration

The Commission
The Commission proposes the Community policy and legislation. It is the executive branch of the EEC. The Commission is responsible for bringing any breaches of the Treaties before the European Court. The Commission sends its proposals to Parliament, which then delivers an opinion. The Commission then informs the parties of remedies they need to implement in respect of the breach.

The European Court of Justice
The court is very influential and the decisions it makes binds the courts of Member States. The court itself is not bound by its own previous decisions, but these could be of persuasive value. When

Community law conflicts with national law, the European Court of Justice has clearly stated that Community law must prevail. The English courts, therefore, must apply such law, even if it is at variance with what has been enacted by Parliament. In 1991, the European Court of Justice overruled a UK Act of Parliament, ruling that the Merchant Shipping Act 1988 was in contravention of EC Law.

Procedure of the European Court of Justice

The court sits in Luxembourg and consists of 13 judges and six Advocate Generals. The procedure is different from an English court. An Advocate General sits on the bench with the judges and once the parties have given their views, he will deliver his opinion, which cannot be deliberated upon by the parties. Advocate Generals are responsible for investigating the issue placed before the court. A report is compiled and recommendations made, which the court will consider. The court is not bound by the report or recommendations made by the Advocate Generals; it can act upon them or reject them as it chooses.

Sources of European Community law

The main source of Community law is embodied in the Treaties which established the EC as it is today. Most important is the Treaty of Rome 1957. In 1972 the European Communities Act was incorporated into English law.

Main sources of law

The Council of Ministers, the European Commission and the European Parliament can make law in the form of regulations, directives and decisions.

Regulations

Regulations are made by the Council of Ministers. They are directly applicable in all Member States.

Directives

Directives have much less influence. The national authorities have a discretion as to the form the directive will take; for example, it could be implemented by an Act of Parliament, or by subordinate legislation.

5

Decisions

Decisions are binding on those to whom they are addressed, this may be an individual, a company or a State. They are created to deal with a particular case.

Non-binding instruments

These include:

Opinions and recommendations
Made under the EC Treaty do not have the force of law. However, they represent statements of EC policy and it could be argued that the Member States should not implement policies at variance with them.

Resolutions, memoranda, guidelines, programmes and communications
Very often the European Commission issues documents detailing actions or procedures being adopted in the Community and laying out the Commission's view on these.

Recommendations and opinions

Recommendations and opinions are not binding at all.

Legislation

Forms of legislation

There are a number of forms of legislation. The most important form is an Act of Parliament. Law is made by the passing of statutes. Until the Act is passed it is known as a bill. The bill must follow a set procedure before it passes into law.

The legislative procedure

- The bill is drafted by lawyers.
- First reading: purely formal, it is read by the clerk of the House, then ordered to be printed.
- Second reading: the general principles of the bill are discussed.
- Committee stage: this is a debate about the bill in detail.
- Report stage: any amendments to the bill are discussed.
- Third reading: final discussion of the amended bill.
- Bill is passed to the House of Lords, goes through the same procedure.
- Royal Assent: bill passes into law and becomes an Act of Parliament.

The Fellicoe procedure was introduced in 1994 to speed up the process of non-contentious Bills through Parliament. The Law of Property (Miscellaneous Provisions) Act 1994, for example, was passed using this faster procedure.

Parliament Acts 1911 and 1949

The House of Lords acts as an important 'checks and balance', considering bills passed to them by the House of Commons. However, the power of the House of Lords to block a bill has been curtailed by the Parliament Acts of 1911 and 1949. Bills can be delayed for a year by the House of Lords, but any 'money bills' which relate purely to financial provisions can be passed without seeking the approval of the House of Lords.

Delegated legislation

Types of legislation
Legislation can be supreme (Acts of Parliament) or subordinate. Subordinate legislation is legislation promulgated by bodies other than Parliament. Because of the complexities of modern society, Parliament is forced to delegate some of its powers to bodies such as local authorities, ministries, etc.

Main types of delegated legislation

Orders In Council
Drafted by Ministers for the Queen's approval.

Statutory instruments
Orders made by Ministers and submitted to Parliament for its approval.

By-laws
By-laws are made by local authorities.

Dangers of delegated legislation

The abuse of power is the chief danger. Parliament attempts to control this by review procedures and delegated legislation can be tested in courts if it is thought to exceed its authority, ie if it has acted *ultra vires* (beyond its powers).

Case law

Case law is made by judges, building on existing precedents. It is vague, inconsistent and very ponderous in nature. Sometimes, difficulties can arise when attempting to extract the law from a judgment. However, it does afford flexibility, thus it has the ability to reflect change in society, as opposed to the rigidity of statute law.

2 The legal profession

The legal profession

The political climate of the 1980s, which was rooted in free competition and *laissez-faire* idealism, necessitated a change in the legal profession. The profession witnessed a threat to its established monopolies as the Government called for greater public accountability and service. The hold the profession had over providing a specific type of legal service was broken and thrown open by changes brought about by Part II of the Courts and Legal Services Act 1990. To fully understand the implications of this legislation it is necessary to first examine the branches of the legal profession.

Barristers

The legal profession has always been a divided one with a medical definition being used to describe the two main branches of barristers and solicitors. Barristers are described as the consultant specialists of the legal profession. They are 'called to the Bar' after keeping term at one of the four Inns: the Inner Temple; the Middle Temple; Lincoln's Inn and Gray's Inn. The General Council of the Bar, established in 1987, is the governing body of barristers. The Council of Legal Education is responsible for the education and examination of intended barristers.

Nature of the work

Barristers specialise in advocacy and can appear in any court or tribunal. They once had the sole privilege of rights of audience in the higher courts; however, the Courts and Legal Services Act 1990 has changed this by introducing new guidelines on who can undertake advocacy work. A barrister's work is not predominantly concerned with advocacy; a number of barristers spend their time writing opinions on specific specialised areas of law to aid solicitors, and in drafting documents.

Barristers are sole practitioners, they do not form partnerships. They practice in offices known as chambers, sharing the expenses with other barristers. The common law rule which prevented barristers from forming multi-disciplinary practices with other professional bodies has been overturned by the Courts and Legal Services Act 1990. However, the General Council of the Bar can still object to barristers engaging in this. There are about 8,935 self-employed barristers in England and Wales (also up to 4,000 who are salaried employees). The most senior barrister in chambers is known as the Head of Chambers and is responsible for the efficient running of the practice. Barristers operate under the 'cab rank' rule which means that any work that is offered to a barrister in his field of practice must be accepted if the barrister is available to undertake it.

The barrister's clerk

An important member of chambers is the barrister's clerk, usually shared by all the barristers in chambers. The barrister's clerk secures work for the barrister and negotiates the fee to be charged (legal aid cases apart which are dealt with by the taxing officer of the court). The Barrister's Clerks Association deals with training and entry into the profession.

Queen's Counsel

There are two types of barrister: QCs (Queen's Counsel) and juniors.

After a barrister has practiced for 15–20 years he or she can apply to 'take silk' which entitles him or her to wear a silk gown in court. QCs make up the top 10% of the barristers profession. QCs are appointed by the Queen on the advice of the Lord Chancellor and allows the public and the profession to identify those barristers who have demonstrated supreme skills in advocacy before the High Courts. However, the system whereby 'silks' are selected has come in for criticism over the years with the press asserting that selection depends on 'judicial whispers'. It is to help combat this criticism that a Working Party has been set up by the Bar Council under the Chairmanship of Michael Kalisher QC. The Kalisher Working Party has been asked to look into the methods, procedures and criteria for the appointment of Queen's Counsel and make recommendations. Their report was published in June 1994 and recommended no structural changes in the procedures whereby QC's are selected, but put forward suggestions on how the system could be improved, for example, there should be an open, formal criteria, and appointments should be based on merit with no positive discrimination in respect of ethnic minorities or women.

The future of the Bar

According to a joint report from two committees of the Bar Council, the Work of the Young Bar, young barristers face a 'bleak future'. There are already too many lawyers competing for an ever decreasing amount of work yet more young lawyers are educated each year. There has been an increase in the number of barristers in independent practice from 6,266 in 1989 to 8,935 self-employed (4,000 salaried employees) in 1997. This obviously has grave consequences for the Bar. There is an ever declining work situation caused in part by the fall in the number of criminal cases. In the magistrates' courts only 137,963 indictable cases were handled in the early part of 1993, as compared to 162,029 for the same period in 1992. Another blow to barristers is the introduction of a new system of standard fees for criminal defence work which was introduced in 1993 prompting even greater competition against the Bar. Under the Standard Fee System a barrister will not be paid for travelling or for waiting time, unlike a solicitors agent, who is a major competitor of the barrister. There is also increased competition from solicitors, who will very soon have full rights of audience in all courts. Right of audience will depend on the applicant obtaining a 'certificate of competence' given by the relevant professional body. These certificates can be 'full' which allows the person holding the certificate to practice in all courts, or it could be a limited one which restricts audience to the lower courts.

The changing Bar

Because of the threats of competition the Bar is in a state of change and is examining its own working practices to determine where change can be made to improve the service and promote the image of the barrister. In 1990 a new Code of Conduct was introduced. This, *inter alia*, relaxed restrictions on advertising, tightened up the 'cab-rank' rule of practice and permitted barristers to work from home instead of in chambers.

A new equality policy has been introduced to ensure women and those from ethnic minorities do not suffer indirect discrimination. Section 64 of the Courts and Legal Services Act 1990 has prohibited sex discrimination. There have long been complaints about discrimination from women and black barristers. In 1983 the Bar set up a Race Relations Committee and in 1986 they accepted guidelines on practices for pupillages and tenancies. Section 64 of the Courts and Legal Services Act 1990 regulates offers of pupillage, tenancies and the distribution of work in chambers. This is important since one-third of the Bar is made up from women and 6% of members are from ethnic minority backgrounds. The Bar is also to introduce a new selection process whereby applicants must undertake an aptitude test as well as satisfying the other necessary qualifying criteria.

Solicitors

Solicitors are known as the 'general practitioners' of the legal profession. Their full title is 'Solicitor of the Supreme Court'. The Law Society figures for 1997 state that there are 87,081 solicitors practising in England and Wales.

Training

The traditional and most usual route to qualify as a solicitor is to take a first degree in law (LLB), with a further year undertaking the Legal Practice Course. Intending solicitors then have to undertake a two year traineeship (which was previously known as articles). A non-law graduate sits the Common Professional Examination (CPE). This allows non-law graduates to qualify the same way as law graduates. It is possible, also, to enter the profession through the Institute of Legal

Executives, as a Legal Executive, sitting the Solicitors Final Examination. In 1995, 8,576 students graduated in law from university. A further 8,000 undertook a one year legal practice course. The number of training contracts available every year in the profession, however, is shrinking (approximately 4,500).

Nature of the work

A solicitor can choose to practice on his own, or to practice with other solicitors in a partnership. They are, however, not allowed to set up partnerships with other professionals. Section 66 of the Courts and Legal Services Act 1990 did abolish the prohibition on solicitors setting up multi-disciplinary practices, but it does not prevent the Law Society ruling against it and preventing those partnerships being formed. The nature of the work of solicitors is extremely varied; they offer a broad spectrum of legal services, such as drawing up contracts, accident claims, drafting partnership deals, matrimonial work, forming companies, conveyancing and probate work, etc. They are responsible for the preparatory pre-court work, including the gathering together of evidence and interviewing clients and witnesses. A solicitor is permitted to appear in front of the magistrates' court, the county court and in front of tribunals in order to represent his client.

The Law Society

The governing body for solicitors is the Law Society, which is responsible for education and training, the regulation of conduct of solicitors, issuing practice certificates and dealing with complaints against solicitors. When representing a client who may need to appear in a High Court, a solicitor must consult a barrister. However, the Courts and Legal Services Act has established guidelines for new advocacy rights for solicitors which will extend their rights of audience to the higher courts. It used to be the case that barristers did not enter into a contract with a solicitor when being briefed by the solicitor regarding a case. This meant that the barrister could not sue the solicitor if he failed to pay the barristers fee. Section 61 of the Courts and Legal Services Act has abolished the common law rule that a barrister cannot enter into a contract for his services. However, the General Council is still able to prohibit barristers from entering such contracts.

Solicitors and barristers enjoy judicial immunity from negligence in respect of a case in court or work which was preparatory to it. Section 62 of the Courts and Legal Services Act reinforces this common law immunity and holds out the protection to other individuals who are lawfully providing a legal service.

Solicitors and the changing legal profession

There has taken place a fundamental change in the legal profession with the solicitors role being altered substantially. The extension of legal services being offered to other professional bodies has eroded, to some extent, the traditional monopolies that existed for the legal profession. The need for public accountability and improved service has led to a radical review of practice management standards and working standards. Practice management standards have been published by the Law Society's Council in April 1993 after consultation with the legal profession, to aid solicitors to effect changes and improve management practices. There existed strict rules governing the practices by which solicitors advertised their services. This has undergone some changes over the years and solicitors can now advertise in newspapers or on radio. With the increase of new technology, solicitors have become more efficient and have streamlined their working environment introducing fax machines and computers. They have also developed larger practices with solicitors engaging in more specialised areas of commercial work. This change has come about in order to combat the onslaught of banks and building societies who offered fast efficient and cheaper conveyancing services than solicitors, attracting the public away from the profession in these matters.

Legal services

The consumer orientated policy of the 1980s has necessitated the profession changing to compete with other professional bodies who are willing to provide an efficient service at a lower cost. The Law Society in the 1980s introduced new conveyancing guidelines to speed up the process and reduce costs. It also scrupulously tries to ensure that licensed conveyancers provide high standards of service. In its attempt to protect solicitors the Law Society has pledged to limit the number of licensed probate practitioners by laying down stringent operational practices. It has further attempted to improve the image of the profession in the eyes of the public by introducing a master profession indemnity insurance and has developed further the Solicitors' Complaints Bureau. The government has also introduced a Legal Services Ombudsman who compliments the Law Society Complaints Bureau.

The 'client care' rules

The 'client care' rules introduced under the Solicitors Practice Rules 1990, lays down guidelines on reducing public criticism. The rules are an attempt to enhance the relationship with the client so that the client is consulted about the steps being taken by the solicitor and is given sufficient information to enable him to report to the appropriate body if he thinks the solicitor is not dealing with the matter properly. The solicitor must now, for example, inform the client of the hourly charging rate. Complaints regarding solicitors are now dealt with by the Office of Supervision of Solicitors (OFSOL) which has taken over from the solicitors complaints bureau.

Changes in education and training

The education and training of solicitors is undergoing change. In September 1993 the Law Society Finals Course was replaced by the new Legal Practice Course. The new course places an emphasis on skills training for new solicitors, whereby they will be better equipped to fulfil their training contracts gaining a more thorough training period. The education and training of solicitors no longer stops when the solicitor begins to practice. All solicitors who have entered the profession after 1987 are required to take further training and must do so until they stop practising. A one-day course has been made compulsory (Professional Development Course) and this has to be completed one year after the new solicitor qualifies, and all solicitors must undertake a management training course approved by the Law Society. There is a worrying trend that we are producing too many law graduates with the consequence that fewer than half who pass the LPC actually gain training contracts. The Lord Chancellor's Advisory Committee on Legal Education and Conduct has put forward proposals for change in legal education, one being a common training programme for both branches of the profession.

Discrimination in the profession

The Royal Commission on Legal Services found both sex and race discrimination in the profession. The Law Society's Annual Statistical Report showed that although there is a greater influx of women into the profession, fewer women become partners in law firms. The RCLS' report highlighted discrimination of ethnic minority groups who were still under-represented in the profession and ethnic minority candidates were less successful at securing training contracts than white candidates.

Legal executives

The modern Institute of Legal Executives (ILEX) was established in 1963 and is the governing body for legal executives. They provide training, a career structure, and set examinations for solicitors staff. Approximately 3,000 students enrol each year with the Institute from very varied backgrounds, from young students with GCSE qualifications to a more mature adult with long-standing clerical experience in a solicitors' office.

The role
Legal executives play an important role, usually being involved in one or more specialised areas such as probate, trust work, conveyancing, matrimonial or civil and criminal litigation. They are employed by a solicitor but they cannot become a partner because they hold no rights of practice. They can, however, deal very comprehensively with the client, from start to finish, and they can manage branch offices and sign cheques on behalf of their firm. They have no rights of audience but can appear in front of a judge on uncontested matters.

Training
Legal executives undertake a two-part training scheme. Part I introduces the student to law, covering a broad introduction to the main areas that solicitors deal with. Part II is a higher level and students study four subjects which will permit them to specialise in the particular area of law they are seeking employment in. If a student wishes to qualify as a Fellow of the Institute of Legal Executives, they have to be aged 25 or over, and have to have had five years' experience in legal practice.

Qualifying as solicitors

The ILEX examination allows many non-law graduates to qualify as solicitors. Their studies exempt them from certain parts of the academic stage of the Law Society's training scheme.

Promoting change

The legal profession was severely criticised as being elitist, restrictive and monopolistic. Labour back benchers expressed dissatisfaction with the high fees charged by the legal profession for conveyancing services. A Royal Commission on Legal Services reported in 1979

(Cmnd 7648) and appeared satisfied with the profession as a whole, recommending little change. The fusion of the profession was considered but rejected; it did not recommend extended rights of audience for solicitors.

The legal profession settled again and it was thought that any further discussion of changes to the structure of the profession was negated. But this was not the case, because in 1983, just four years later, in the House of Commons a second reading was given to Austin Mitchell's Private Members Bill which was advocating the abolition of the long held monopoly of solicitors over conveyancing. The 'House Buyers Bill' was withdrawn by Mr Mitchell when the government agreed to allow legislation to permit non-solicitors to undertake conveyancing services, providing they underwent proper training and proper standards were maintained to protect the public.

Licensed conveyancers

The Administration of Justice Act 1985, Part II, led the way for licensed conveyancers to practice. The Building Societies Act 1986 permitted banks and building societies to offer conveyancing services to clients who were not already borrowing from them as lenders. However, these provisions were never implemented.

Threat of competition

This stance taken by the government completely surprised the legal profession. The threat of competition to solicitors' rights of audience over conveyancing forced them to challenge the demarcation lines drawn between them and the Bar's monopoly over rights of audience in higher courts. This infuriated the Bar and a deep schism between members was much commented upon.

A Committee was set up in 1986 chaired by Lady Marre. The Committee which was made up of solicitors and barristers looked at the legal profession and how changes could be made to the provision of legal services. In 1988 the Committee agreed that solicitors should have extended rights of audience and also should be able to be appointed as High Court judges. However, the profession was still clearly divided over these issues and no clear agreement was reached through the Committee. The Government decided in 1989 that radical reform of the profession was necessary.

The Green Paper

The Lord Chancellor declared that he was to introduce a Green Paper, 'The Work and Organisation of the Legal Profession' (Cmnd 570), which laid out the proposals for reform. This was published in 1989 and was a reinforcement of the government's commitment to a *laissez-faire* doctrine for the provision of legal services, which had to be competitive, orientated towards the consumer, and carried out by skilled professionals.

Proposals for reform

There was to be an end to the monopoly, long held by the Bar, over the rights of audience in higher courts. All new practitioners would have to gain a certificate of competence. This would be either a full certificate, giving advocacy in all courts, or a limited certificate, which gave rights of advocacy in the magistrates' court, county court and Crown Court (where no jury was sitting). Solicitors were to be permitted to form multi-disciplinary partnerships, and barristers were to be allowed to take instructions direct from the public rather than waiting to be briefed by a solicitor. Further, contingency fees were to be introduced whereby lawyers could undertake cases on a 'no win, no fee' basis.

Responses to the Green Paper

The response to the Green Papers was very varied. The Bar, in 'Quality of Justice', declared that it would be in the best interests of the public if they were served by an independent Bar. The Law Society's response was to reject the proposals, in 'Striking a Balance', and they warned that there was danger in permitting too much government power in the regulation of legal services. The judges also declared the proposals dangerous; they feared that the judiciary would be undermined by this concentration of government power over the profession.

The White Paper

A White Paper was published in July 1989, forming the basis of the Courts and Legal Services Act 1990. This demonstrated clearly that the government had listened to some of the criticisms levied at the Green Paper. The Act received the Royal Assent in 1990.

Implementations under the Courts and Legal Services Act 1990

Section 17

This provides for 'the development of legal services in England and Wales'. It refers to the development of 'advocacy litigation, conveyancing and probate services'. The concern is with the proper and adequate supervision of those persons providing these services and that they comply with criteria laid down to regulate their activities, for example, provisions for a proper system of complaints and adequate insurance in order to protect consumers.

Regulation of non-solicitors

The Act allows for the regulation and authorisation of non-solicitors to provide conveyancing services, such as licensed conveyancers. The Act also under ss 34 and 35 sets up an Authorised Conveyancing Practitioners' Board. The Board has a Chairman and four to eight other members who are appointed by the Lord Chancellor, who will consider, *inter alia*:

(A) Appointing persons who have experience in, or knowledge of:

    (1) the provision of conveyancing services;

    (2) financial arrangements associated with conveyancing;

    (3) consumer affairs; and

(B) Securing, so far as is reasonably practicable, that the composition of the Board is such as to provide a proper balance between the interests of authorised practitioners and those who make use of their services.

(s 34(3) of the CLSA 1990)

Regulatory bodies

Three bodies regulating conveyancing:

- The Authorised Conveyancing Practitioners' Board
- The Law Society (which will guide firms of solicitors)
- Council for Licensed Conveyancers

The Board will be concerned with the responsibility of regulating persons, or bodies, providing conveyancing services, making sure that they are fit to provide the service and have taken out adequate insurance cover which may be necessary to compensate clients. All applicants must apply for membership of the Conveyancing Ombudsman Scheme (s 37 of the CLSA 1990).

Section 40

This deals with the regulation, competency and conduct of authorised practitioners. The Lord Chancellor has the power to make any provisions he thinks to be necessary with respect to:

(A)   maintaining satisfactory standards of competence and conduct in connection with the provision by them of conveyancing services;

(B)   that in providing such service (and in particular in fixing their charges) they act in a manner which is consistent with the maintenance of fair competition between authorised practitioners and others providing conveyancing services; and

(C)   that the interests of their clients are satisfactorily protected.

(s 40(1) of the CLSA 1990)

Section 41

Section 41 introduces a Conveyancing Appeals Tribunal which will hear appeals from anyone who is not satisfied by the decision of the Board.

Section 43

Section 43 sets up a conveyancing Ombudsman who will deal with complaints against authorised practitioners. It is the duty of every authorised practitioner to be a member of this scheme.

Section 45

Section 45 allows for the Director General of Fair Trading to discuss the rules and regulations of the Board and advise the Lord Chancellor whether the rules or regulations would restrict, prevent or distort competition in any way.

Section 46

Section 46 provides investigating powers for the Board.

Section 47

Section 47 provides the power to obtain information and require the production of documents.

Section 51

Section 51 gives the Board intervention powers.

Section 53

Section 53 provides for the Council for Licensed Conveyancers to be a recognised authorised body, and to grant rights of audience to licensed conveyancers to allow them to undertake litigation etc.

Probate services

The Act allows for banks, building societies and insurance companies to apply for grants of probate. It also permits professional bodies to apply to the Lord Chancellor to become 'Approved Bodies' who may grant their members the right to offer probate services. However, an Approved Body can only do this if the members:

(A)   business is, and is likely to continue to be, carried on by fit and proper persons or, in the case of an individual, that he is a fit and proper person;

(B)   that he, and any person employed by him in the provision of probate services, is suitably trained;

(C)   that satisfactory arrangements will at all times be in force for covering adequately the risk of any claim made against him in connection with the provision of probate services by him, however arising.

Rights of audience

Since the Green Papers in 1989, attention has focused on the proposals for ending barristers' monopoly of rights of audience in the higher courts. This onslaught by solicitors on the Bar's long-standing monopoly was greeted with much consternation. There was criticism of the solicitors' ability to undertake this and justifications put forward by the Bar for the retention of their fundamental right to audience in the higher courts. For example, they argued that if solicitors were to gain rights of audience in the Crown Court this would drastically reduce the work available for young barristers who were predominantly supported by this. They doubted whether solicitors would be able to gain the requisite skill in advocacy necessary to conduct a case before higher courts, and if they did master the skill, they doubted whether they would be able to maintain it.

The Marre Committee

The profession became embroiled in a heated debate as to whether the Bar should lose its traditional right of audience in the higher courts. The Marre Committee was set up to consider the Future of the Legal Profession, looking into legal education, the legal profession and legal services. In 1988 it recommended that solicitors ought to have the right of audience in higher courts and should be permitted to be appointed as High Court judges.

Legal services

Section 17

The Act embodies a statutory objective and a general principle to help those providing legal services to offer better provisions. The statutory objective is:

... the development of legal services in England and Wales (and in particular the development of advocacy, litigation, conveyancing and probate services) by making a provision for new or better ways of providing such services and a wider choice of person providing them, while maintaining the proper and efficient administration of justice.

(s 17 of the CLSA 1990)

The general principle is that rights of audience and the right to conduct litigation should only be granted if the person is adequately trained and qualified to undertake it, with commitment to a code of conduct in respect of advocacy (particularly important being a principle of non-discrimination (3)(C), similar to the 'cab-rank' principle, which the Bar would like to see extended to all provisions of legal services). However, solicitors argue this would be unworkable and are resisting attempts for this to be implemented.

Section 27

Section 27 sets out the guidelines for rights of audience and rights to conduct litigation. Barristers retain the rights of audience in all courts and solicitors continue to have rights of audience already exercisable by them.

Solicitors' rights of audience

There has now been approval by the Lord Chancellor and senior judges for the rules under which solicitors are allowed extended rights of audience. Solicitors can apply for the grant of higher courts qualifications for civil or criminal proceedings. The higher courts (criminal proceedings) qualifications allow for rights of audience in the Crown Court in all proceedings and in other courts in all criminal proceedings. The higher courts (civil proceedings) qualification allows audience in the High Court in all proceedings and in other courts in all civil proceedings. To obtain the higher courts qualification the solicitor must have practised for three years. The criteria for obtaining these qualifications is, *inter alia*, experience in advocacy in the higher courts for at least two years before applying, and the completion of an advocacy training course.

In 1997 the Lord Chancellor gave his approval to the Law Society for rights of audience in the higher courts for employed solicitors, this was given, however, with conditions attached. Solicitors will apply individually for the rights, undertaking the necessary tests before they are granted. Employed solicitors will not be granted the right to appear on their own as advocates in certain situations, for example, prosecutions in criminal proceedings which have been committed to the Crown Court. The Higher Courts Qualification Regulations 1992 govern the granting of solicitors' advocacy rights. In July 1996 the number of solicitors achieving the higher courts qualification totalled 420, thus only a small percentage of solicitors are exercising their right to the higher qualification. In December 1994 the Lord Chancellor's Advisory Committee on Legal Education and Conduct tendered research to establish whether granting greater rights of audience to solicitors would enhance the provision of legal services. Research from Bristol University, Faculty of Law, found, *inter alia*, that it is in the area of criminal law that 'extended rights of audience would be most significant'. Yet, they argue that, even so, there was no real apparent threat to barristers in this area. Solicitors lacked the flexibility of barristers in terms of their work structure and inflexible Crown Court listings makes it difficult for solicitors to compete with the Bar ((1997) 14 *New Law Journal* 212).

End of the Bar's monopoly

Since the autumn of 1995 more solicitors have been able to gain rights of audience in the higher courts after successfully completing the Law Society Training Course. Whether the Bar's monopoly has been broken, however, is doubtful. In fact it is argued that the threat to the whole legal profession which the CLSA proposed has not been realised.

3 Judges and judicial reasoning

> **You should be familiar with the following areas:**
> - the appointment and tenure of judges
> - the independence of the judiciary
> - judicial offices
> - the training of judges
> - lay justices and stipendiary magistrates
> - case law and judicial reasoning
> - statutory interpretation
> - interpreting EC law

The training of judges

Judges in the UK receive very little training, although there are seminar programmes for the training of assistant recorders. The issue of training for judges was considered, *inter alia*, by the Runciman Committee who recommended that judges should be compelled to attend refresher courses, that more resources should be made available for the training of judges, and that people from a variety of agencies should be involved throughout the criminal justice system. They also suggested that judges should be subject to some form of appraisal by leading judges. Indeed, many commentators are calling for more accountability from the judiciary. The Law Society and Liberty have put forward the idea of a 'Judicial Commission' to monitor judges and promote more public accountability and scrutiny, however, many senior judges do not agree with this total judicial accountability that they argue could never be achieved.

Appointment and tenure

The Act of Settlement 1700 laid down the statutory foundation for the appointment of judges. Judges held office *quamdiu se bene gesserint* (if they were of good behaviour). This gave judges security of tenure, and they could be removed only upon address of both Houses of Parliament. However, no English judge has been removed under this procedure. This security of tenure available to the superior judge is not enjoyed by circuit judges or recorders; they can be removed by the Lord Chancellor for misbehaviour or incapacity.

The independence of the judiciary

Judges must be completely impartial when applying the law and should not allow any political favour or bias to influence their judgment. The idea of the independence of the judiciary from the state is important to the legal system; protection from removal and the doctrine of judicial immunity reinforces this. Much stress is laid upon the constitutional importance of the independence of judges, and accords with Montesquieu's theory of the separation of the powers. To maintain the idea of non-political interference, judges cannot be Members of Parliament. However, the Lord Chancellor's position is rather incongruous, having a foot in both camps – being a political appointee and member of the government. Judicial immunity from civil suit protects superior judges in respect of their activities during the course of judicial office.

Social background of the judiciary

The judiciary is criticised because its members are usually drawn from a very elite social background, mostly from public schools and Oxford or Cambridge universities. They are from upper middle class origins, and it is suggested that because of this and their isolation from life within society they are out of touch with the moral values of the generation they are trying and sentencing.

Appointment and selection

It is argued that the present system of appointment and selection of judges is discriminatory to women and ethnic minority groups. The Lord Chancellor in 'Development in Judicial Appointment Procedures' 1994, has advocated that more judges should be appointed from these groups, and he has developed proposals to stimulate applications from these unrepresented groups. Further, posts for circuit and district judges would be advertised in the national press. Candidates would be interviewed by a panel which would contain a serving judge and a lay member. This system will eventually be extended to judicial posts up to High Court level.

The House of Commons Home Affairs Committee into Judicial Appointments Procedures June 1996, found that there was no need for large scale alterations to the judicial appointments system. The under-representation of women at higher level was thought not to be helped by introducing positive discrimination. Also rejected by the committee was the use of open advertising and it was in full favour of senior judges being appointed by invitation only through secret negotiations with high ranking judges and key figures from the Bar.

Judicial offices

The Lord High Chancellor

The Lord High Chancellor presides over the House of Lords in its judicial capacity. Though it is a committee of the House of Lords, the court is separate.

Lord Chief Justice

The Lord Chief Justice is the second most senior judge. He is the senior judge of the Queen's Bench Division of the High Court.

Master of the Rolls

The Master of the Rolls presides over the Civil Division of the Court of Appeal and can also sit in the Criminal Division. He is responsible for admitting newly qualified solicitors to the Roll of the court which allows them to practice. He is appointed by the Queen on the advice of the Prime Minister.

Vice Chancellor

The Vice Chancellor is in charge of the day to day running of the Chancery Division of the High Court.

The Lords of Appeal in Ordinary

Life peers will either have held high judicial office for two years or more, or they will have been practising barristers or advocates for at least 15 years. They comprise the House of Lords (court) and they hear civil and criminal appeals on issues of public importance. Their decisions bind all the lower courts, but not necessarily the House of Lords itself. Under the Administration of Justices Act up to 11 Lords of Appeal in ordinary are permitted. They are appointed under s 6 of the Appellate Jurisdiction Act 1876 (amended s 71 of the CLSA 1990).

Lord Justices of Appeal

There are 27 Lords Justices of Appeal. They are usually appointed from High Court judges. They staff both the Civil Division and the Criminal Division of the Court of Appeal.

High Court judges

High Court judges are allocated to work in any of the three divisions of the High Court. They are chosen from the ranks of circuit judges of two years' standing, or from those with a High Court qualification under the Courts and Legal Services Act 1990.

Circuit judges

Circuit judges are part-time judges of the Crown Court. They are appointed from the ranks of barristers or solicitors of 10 years' standing.

District judges

Under s 74 of the CLSA 1990, county court registrars are now known as district judges. They have limited judicial power, and are appointed from practising lawyers with at least seven years' standing.

Magistrates

Lay justices

Lay justices sit in magistrates' courts, they are part-time and are unpaid, receiving only expenses. They try the majority of minor criminal offences, approximately 98% of all criminal cases are processed through the magistrates' court, as well as having some civil jurisdiction.

Lay justices are vital to the legal system as they provide a cheap and quick system of justice. They are appointed by the Lord Chancellor from individuals put forward by local organisations. They must be between 21 and 60 years of age, and, usually must live or work in the particular area.

Unlike superior judges magistrates are not subject to the doctrine of judicial independence; many are local councillors or business people. Though a balance is attempted to ensure certain groups in the population are represented, many groups are in fact excluded. Magistrates are predominantly drawn from middle class males in the community and this imbalance causes concern. There are not enough women magistrates or members of ethnic minority groups. Research by Baldwin (1976) showed this tendency to be very prevalent and the feeling is that magistrates are not a true representation of the community.

Stipendiary magistrates

The term 'magistrates' incorporates the professional stipendiary magistrate as well as the lay justices of the peace. Stipendiary magistrates are paid, usually barristers or solicitors. They preside over busy courts in large cities where the use of lay magistrates would be impracticable. Stipendiary magistrates, unlike lay justices, can sit alone.

The justice's clerk

Lay magistrates can only sit if they have a qualified clerk to assist them. He advises the justices as to the law and practice; however, he is not allowed to interfere with their decision. The clerk is salaried, usually a barrister or solicitor of seven years' standing.

Case law and judicial precedent

A prominent element of common law is the principle of *stare decisis* (let the decision stand). It is common to speak today of law being 'judge made'. Judges, when deciding a case before them, must consider previous cases and take account of how previous judges have dealt with similar cases. Therefore, the court starts from a foundation of principles which are already in existence and tries to find a solution in line with principles that have previously been decided. A distinctive characteristic of the law is this judicial development of principle. The traditional role of the judge is not to make law but to decide cases using existing legal principles, they are bound to do this. It is suggested that when a judge reaches his decision he is only stating what the common law has always been. However, if a judge has to make a point of law which has never come before the courts then surely the judge is creating law, not merely enforcing what the law states. In *Shaw v DPP* (1961) their Lordships held that there is such an offence as 'conspiracy to corrupt public morals' the House of Lords thus extended the criminal law. Many new rules of equity have been developed in recent years. One example is the principle of equitable estoppel in *Central London Property Trust Ltd v High Trees House Ltd* (1947). Lord Denning in *Gourier v Union of Post Office Workers* (1977) had to deliberate on a point that had never been looked at before and he declared that it was for the judge to state what the law is:

Parliament has passed no enactment on it, there is no binding precedent in our books on it. It is a new thing. Whenever a new situation arises which has not been considered before, the judges have to say what the law is. In doing so, we do not change the law, we declare it. We consider it on principle, and then pronounce on it. As the old writers quaintly put it, the law lies 'in the breast of the judges'.

See also *Jones v Secretary of State for Social Services* (1972) (*per* Lord Simon).

Hierarchy of courts

The doctrine of judicial precedent depends on the hierarchy of the courts for its operation, a court is bound by a decision of a court above it and usually by a previous decision of its own.

The House of Lords binds all lower courts, the Court of Appeal (Civil Division) binds all lower courts and usually itself, the Court of Appeal (Criminal Division) binds all lower courts; the High Court binds all lower courts; the county courts bind nobody; similarly the magistrates' courts and all others bind nobody.

In the 1970s Lord Denning, who was head of the Civil Division of the Court of Appeal tried to establish that the Court of Appeal could, if it wanted to, choose not to follow a decision of the House of Lords if it was *per incuriam*, or out of date (*cessante ratione, cosset upsa lex*). However, this was frowned upon by his colleagues and he was chastised by the House of Lords. The Court of Appeal must follow a House of Lords decision (*Cassell v Broome* (1972); *Rookes v Bamard* (1964)).

The most important decisions are those of the House of Lords, its decisions bind the Court of Appeal, all divisions of the High Court and all inferior courts. Up until 1966 the House of Lords was bound by its own previous decisions. However, after the 1966 Practice Statement by

Lord Gardiner this has been changed. The House of Lords would treat its previous decisions as normally binding, however, it would be able to depart from a previous decision if it decided it was proper to do so.

As we have seen, the Court of Appeal (Civil Division) is bound by decisions of the House of Lords and bound by its own previous decisions unless there are exceptional circumstances:

- unless the previous decision conflicts with a later House of Lords decision;
- unless the decision is given *per incuriam*; and
- where the decision conflicts with another previous decision of the Court of Appeal (*Young v Bristol Aeroplane Co* (1944)).

The High Court

In *C (a minor) v DPP* (1994) the Divisional Court decided that they could depart from the earlier Divisional Court decision and declared that there is no longer a presumption that a minor aged between 10 and 14 is incapable of committing a crime.

Court of Justice of the European Communities

Section 3(1) of the European Communities Act 1972 states that with regard to legal proceedings in the UK, questions as to the validity of the Treaty of Rome must be decided in accordance with the jurisprudence of the European Court of Justice. Thus the British courts are bound by the decisions of the European Court.

Statutory interpretation

Interpretation of statutes plays an important role in the life of a judge. It is not always easy for courts to interpret Acts of Parliament. When problems of construction arise judges have to use their traditional skills to resolve them. The decision of the House of Lords in *Pepper v Hart* (1993) means that judges, to aid their interpretation, can take into account reports of Hansard to help clarify ambiguous legislation. They can also refer to the European Commission's explanatory memoranda (*travaux preparatoires*) when dealing with issues of EC law. There is no actual Act of Parliament to guide judges regarding the interpretation of the Acts. The Interpretation Act 1978 gives some assistance in defining key words and phrases. As more of our law becomes statute based the interpretation of these statutes is a central feature of the role of a judge. Words can portray many meanings. Professor Hart has referred to the 'spoken case of settled meanings of words and the penumbral area of doubt'.

Interpreting statute law

There are considerable problems involved in judicial interpretation of Acts of Parliament. These problems are constant and recurring, and sometimes cause controversy. Judges have taken different stances in respect of statutory interpretation. A tentative approach by the House of Lords can be identified during the early post-war period, judges favouring the literal application of the law. This circumspect approach, however, has wavered, and judges have been more adventurous in influencing the law as opposed to merely applying the strict meaning of a statute; Lord Denning, it could be argued, being numbered against the most creative in this respect. The fundamental principle of statutory interpretation is that it is for the court to interpret the true intention of the legislator. While Parliament provides the legal framework, it is the courts that must fill in the gaps, omissions, or make clear ambiguous words. All Acts of Parliament are complex, even though the policy is for drafting statutes in simple English. To aid the layman to interpret the Act, a section on interpretation is included. Further, there is the Interpretation Act 1978 which gives guidelines to help with interpretation.

Traditional rules of statutory interpretation

When statutory words are ambiguous judges can use rules of construction to assist them in determining what Parliament had intended. There are three main rules of statutory interpretation.

The literal rule

This rule states that simple words which have an obvious everyday meaning should be given that meaning by the courts. This approach to interpretation has been criticised because if a statute is very ambiguous, the end result may be completely out of step with what Parliament actually intended. The literal rule, it is argued, is very outdated and hinders rather than aids interpretation. Lord Denning in *Engineering Industry Training Board v Samual Talbot Ltd* (1969) stated:

... we no longer construe Acts of Parliament according to their literal meaning. We construe them according to their object and intent.

The mischief rule

This is sometimes known as the rule in *Heydons Case* (1584). Here the courts look to the purpose of the Act and try to interpret the Act in order to fulfil that purpose. Four stages need to be considered:

- What was the common law before the making of the Act?
- What was the mischief or defect for which the common law did not provide?
- What remedy did Parliament provide?
- The true reason for the remedy.

Simonds and Denning LJJ's approach in *Magnor and St Mellans v Newport Corporation* (1952) is worth comparing.

The mischief rule is arguably the most important of the rules. In *Rogers v Dodd* (1968) it was a condition of a coffee-bars registration under the Brighton Corporation Act 1966 that it should close at 1.00 am. Although the coffee-bar had closed its doors they were still serving snacks through an open window at 1.40 am. The question to be determined was whether the coffee-bar was in fact still 'open'. Lord Parker applied the mischief rule and stated:

It seems to me that the mischief aimed at by the Act of 1966 is the congregation of the public in premises where no doubt they are served with refreshments, and where abuses are likely to occur in the sense of undue noise to the neighbourhood, peddling of drugs and other such matters.

Lord Parker had applied the mischief rule to an earlier case *Smith v Hughes* (1960) where two women were convicted of soliciting contrary to the Street Offences Act 1959. The women were tapping on a window to try to attract passers by. It was perfectly evident that they were soliciting, the question was whether they were soliciting in a street or public place. Lord Parker stated:

For my part I approach the matter by considering what is the mischief aimed at by this Act. Everybody knows that this was an Act intended to clean up the streets, to enable people to walk along the streets without being molested or solicited by common prostitutes. Viewed in that way, it can matter little whether the prostitute is soliciting while in the street, or is standing in the doorway or on a balcony or at a window or whether the window is shut or open or half-open in each case her solicitation is projected to and addressed to somebody walking in the street.

The golden rule

This rule states that where words in a statute are ambiguous, the meaning given should be the one that is closest to what Parliament intended. This rule is applied widely to avoid an absurdity. In *Luke v Inland Revenue Commissioners* (1963) Lord Reid stated that:

To apply the words literally is to defeat the obvious intention of the legislation and to produce a wholly unreasonable result. To achieve the obvious intention and produce a reasonable result we must do some violence to the words. This is not a new problem though our standard of drafting is such that it rarely emerges. The general principle is well settled. It is only where the words are absolutely incapable of a construction which will accord with the apparent intention of the provision and will avoid a wholly unreasonable result that the words of the enactment must prevail.

A further example can be seen in *Re Sigsworth* (1935) where the rule was used to overrule the common law rule under the Administration of Estates Act 1925.

The introduction of *Pepper v Hart* has opened the way to the purposive approach to statutory interpretation which is increasingly favoured by the judiciary. The interpretation of European law has necessitated that judges consider domestic and European law together. Judges have given a purposive interpretation of EC law and appear to have adopted this method as favoured over the literal rule (*Lister v Forth Dry Dock* (1989)). The abandoning of the literal rule and looking to the spirit of the law is not a new initiative, many judges already adopt a purposive approach – Lord Denning in *Davis v Johnson* (1979) for example.

Maxims of interpretation

Ejusdem generis

Categories of words, classes of persons, will be referred to only if they fall within the category listed.

Noscitur a sociis

Words within a section will be read in their context.

Expressio unius exclusio alterus

This means that if there is a specific member of a class mentioned it will exclude other members.

Intrinsic aids

- The title of an Act

  Can be considered. Title can be long or short. Long title can assist in interpreting the aims of the Act.

- Preamble

  Used only if the Act is not clear.

- Headings

  Can be useful aid if the Act is ambiguous.

Presumptions

Parliament is presumed not to overrule certain presumptions, for example, not to alter the common law, not to go against natural justice and not to go against international law etc.

Essentially, the use of these rules can be reduced to whether the judge takes the words used as being interpreted in their everyday meaning, which could lead to an absurd conclusion, or whether the words used should be interpreted in a wider context to result in a more balanced outcome. There is also a further question, should the words be interpreted on their own or as a phrase or complete sentence? Professor Hart in *Definition and Theory in Jurisprudence* (1953, p 8) states that:

Long ago Bentham issued a warning that legal words demanded a special method of elucidation and he enunciated a principle that is the beginning of wisdom in this matter though it is not the end. He said we must never take these words alone, but consider whole sentences in which they play their characteristic role. We must take not the word 'right' but the sentence 'you have a right' not the word 'state' but the sentence 'he is a member of an official of the state'. His warning has largely been disregarded and jurists have continued to hammer away at single words.

This particular problem was highlighted in *Bromley London Borough Council v Greater London Council* (1982).

Further, Michael Zander has stated that:

Ultimately, it may be said that the Law Lords are adopting a more dispassionate cool, uninvolved attitude which gives prime importance to the statutory words and refuses to become embroiled in the policy behind the records. The

Court of Appeal at least when Lord Denning presides, is more inclined to wear its heart on its sleeve, to take a view on the policy of legislation and to shape its decisions by its sense of the equities, there is no way of saying in the abstract which approach is more often likely to produce a sensible result, but there can be no doubt that whereas the Law Lords have adopted a more restrained approach, Lord Denning's way more obviously requires the judge to judge.

(*The Guardian*, 14 December 1979)

Interpreting EC law

The treaties are drafted very broadly. UK courts must interpret the Treaties in line with the principles of the European Court of Justice. The importance here lies in the actual principles and not in the wording of the decisions. When UK courts interpret EC legislation they must adopt the same purpose and principles of the European Court of Justice (*Bulmer v Bollinger* (1974)).

That means not examining words meticulously and not applying a strict literal interpretation. *R v Hern* (1978) is a good example of this.

4 The criminal process

You should be familiar with the following areas:

- the courts and court procedure
- the Royal Commission on Criminal Justice: the Commission's recommendations for reform of the criminal justice system
- the Police and Magistrates' Courts Act
- the investigation of crime
- arrest procedures
- advice at the police station
- interviews: conduct and control
- stop and search
- entry search and seizure

The courts and court procedure

The courts

Some courts deal only with civil cases and some only with criminal. However, for the most part, they can deal with both.

Magistrates' courts

Magistrates' courts deal with criminal cases as follows:

- They try summarily (without a jury) all minor offences and may try offences triable summarily or on indictment with a jury, if the accused consents and the magistrates' court considers that the case is suitable for trial in that court.
- They conduct committal proceedings, which are preliminary investigations of the prosecution case, when the offence is triable only on indictment (by a Crown Court) or if it is an offence triable either

way which it is decided should not be tried summarily. If the magistrates are satisfied they commit the defendant for trial in a Crown Court.

In 1995 an estimated 1.93 million defendants were proceeded against in magistrates' courts. Receipts of cases in magistrates' courts (including those later sent to Crown Court) have fallen by 6% in 1995 (very little change was shown in 1994). Proceedings for defendants finalised dropped by 2% to 1.93 million in 1995. The number of indictable offences dropped by 7% to 437,000 partly due to the fact that in August 1994 changes were made to the charging standards for wounding/assault offences. Summary non-motoring offences were up by 1% to 604,000. Approximately one in five indictable offences (including triable either way) are committed each year for trial or sentence to the Crown Court. Reasons for committing offences to the Crown Court:

- The offence is triable only on indictment and the magistrates' hearing is only a preliminary one.
- The committal is directed by the magistrates, or the defendant has elected for trial at the Crown Court.
- A triable either way offence having been tried summarily results in the court believing that a higher sentence should be imposed thus the defendant is committed to the Crown Court for sentencing.

In certain cases, for example serious fraud, it is possible to by pass committal proceedings, the prosecution serving a notice of transfer.

Maximum penalties

The maximum penalties which magistrates may impose on a defendant convicted summarily of a criminal offence is six months' imprisonment and/or a fine of up to £5,000 (fixed by the Criminal Justice Act 1991). If the defendant is convicted of two or more offences at the same time, the maximum sentence of imprisonment rises to 12 months. If the magistrates feel that they lack the power to sentence a defendant, that the sentence may be inadequate to fit the gravity of the offence, they can commit the defendant to the Crown Court for sentencing.

A defendant convicted of a criminal offence can appeal for a rehearing by a Crown Court. Either the defendant or the prosecution may appeal on a point of law only by way of 'case stated' to a Divisional Court of the Queen's Bench Division. There are approximately 150 such cases every year. Appeal from the Divisional Court is to the House of Lords. Either side may appeal on points of law. However, the

Divisional Court must certify that the point is of general public importance and either that Court or the House of Lords must grant leave to appeal. (These cases are rare – approximately 10 per year.)

Crown Court

The Crown Court tries all indictable offences with a jury and hears appeals and deals with committals for sentencing from magistrates' courts. There is a right of appeal on criminal matters to the criminal division of the Court of Appeal. An appeal by way of 'case stated' on a point of law may also be made to a Divisional Court of the Queen's Bench Division. Except in cases where the Attorney General intervenes then the law is governed by the Criminal Appeal Act 1968; the Court may allow the appeal but can 'apply the proviso', that is, uphold the accused's appeal on the law but retain the conviction on the ground that no miscarriage of justice has occurred (s 2). The accused may only appeal, either against conviction on a point of law, where no leave is required to appeal; or against conviction on a point of fact, where leave is required; or against sentence (again leave is required). Sections 35–36 of the Criminal Justice Act 1988 give the Attorney General the power to refer sentences to the Court of Appeal if he thinks they are too lenient; this power exists only in very serious offences. If the appeal to the House of Lords is on a point of law, either side has the right to appeal. The Court of Appeal must give leave to appeal and certify the point of law is of general public importance.

The High Court

This is structured in three tiers:

- Queen's Bench Division
- Chancery Division
- Family Division

In hearing a case for the first time, a High Court judge sits alone. A Divisional Court of two or more High Court judges sits to hear appeals from magistrates. It also exercises the supervisory jurisdiction of the Queen's Bench Division.

If the Divisional Court decides that the magistrates were wrong, it can reverse or amend the decision; it can remit the case to the magistrates to continue hearing the case or discharge or convict the accused where applicable; or it can make such orders as it considers fit.

Judicial Committee of the House of Lords

Apart from the jurisdiction of the European Court of Justice, the Judicial Committee of the House of Lords is the highest Court of Appeal. It hears appeals from both the civil and the criminal divisions of the Court of Appeal (and in certain circumstances direct from the High Court).

The youth court

Juvenile justice has undergone many changes over the last few years. The initiatives behind these changes have been to reduce the number of young people appearing before the criminal courts and being given a custodial sentence. The use of formal cautioning by the police was fully encouraged and the re-routing of young offenders away from the criminal courts into the care of local authorities and community service programmes. This policy of using the criminal courts as a last resort has been positively reinforced by the Children Act 1989, which has definite guidelines about the way in which juvenile courts deal with young offenders. However, although this philosophy of re-routing young offenders away from the criminal courts met with some success in respect of charging and sentencing of juvenile offenders, there was still an alarmingly high percentage of young offenders being remanded in prisons and remand centres. In his report of HM Chief Inspector of Prisons 1989, Judge Tumin described the conditions in which young offenders were detained as 'highly disturbing'. The government were forced into reviewing the situation, and in the Home Office Consultation paper, 'The Remand of Alleged Juvenile Offenders' (February 1991), they stated they would prevent juvenile offenders from being given custodial remands, unless the juvenile was a danger to society, and expressed the hope to phase out prison remands for juveniles altogether. The Criminal Justice Act (ss 60–62) contains the relevant provisions in this area.

Youth court and remand changes

The juvenile court is now called the youth court dealing with offenders aged between 10 and 17 (Criminal Justice Act 1991). The 1991 Act identifies a number of changes, all of which must be considered in the context of the Children Act 1989. The Criminal Justice Act 1991 prohibits in certain cases the sentencing of juvenile offenders; it lays more emphasis on parental responsibility and stresses the need for more contact with social services and probation officers. The Act focuses on local authority accommodation and secure accommodation for remands of juveniles and prohibits the use of custody for any young offender under the age of 17. Sections 60 and 62 of the 1991 Act amends s 23 of the Children and Young Persons Act 1969. This enables the courts to take control over the conditions of a juvenile remanded in local authority care. The court can:

- insist the juvenile adheres to any condition which may have been imposed under the Bail Act 1976;
- make the local authority take responsibility to ensure that the juvenile offender complies with these requirements (s 23(9)(a));
- insist that the juvenile offender is not placed beside another named person (eg co-defendant) (s 23(9)(b)).

The court, before applying any of these conditions, must consult the local authority and explain the reasons for its decision to the young offender in plain ordinary language so that the young person can understand (s 23(8)).

Secure accommodation

To detain a young person in secure accommodation is a very grave step and all other avenues must be explored before this decision is reached. A secure accommodation order must not be the result of the fact that no other placement was available because of staffing shortages, or as a form of punishment. The aims and objectives of this measure need to be fully explored as being in the best interests of the juvenile offender. A local authority can detain a juvenile in secure accommodation for up to 72 hours within any 28 day period by an administrative decision. If the juvenile is to be detained longer than this period the local authority must apply to the court to grant a secure accommodation order for:

- the maximum period of the remand for when the child is committed to the Crown Court for trial; or
- an order for a maximum of 28 days when the child is committed to the Crown Court for trial.

The criteria for granting a secure accommodation order are set down in s 25 of the Children Act 1989 which states that an order can be made only if it appears:

- that (i) he has a history of absconding and is likely to abscond from any other description of accommodation; and (ii) if he absconds he is likely to suffer significant harm; or

- that if he is kept in any other description of accommodation he is likely to injure himself or other persons.

Where a juvenile is remanded by a court on a serious offence, reg 6 of the Children (Secure Accommodation) Regulations 1991 applies. If he has been charged or convicted of:

- an offence punishable with 14 years' imprisonment or more in the case of an adult; or
- a violent offence (or if he has been previously convicted of a violent offence). A secure accommodation order can be granted only if:
- the child is likely to abscond from non-secure accommodation; or
- the child is likely to injure himself or other people if he is detained in non-secure accommodation.

Section 94 of the Children Act 1989 allows an appeal by the juvenile or the local authority against the granting of a secure accommodation order by the court.

Young offenders aged 14–17 convicted at the Crown Court can be detained for up to the adult maximum, this includes life for offences carrying maximum sentences of 14 years or more in the case of an adult offender, or for the offences of causing death by dangerous driving, causing death by careless driving while under the influence of alcohol or drugs – for those aged 16–17 indecent assault on a female would be included. These provisions have been extended by the Criminal Justice and Public Order Act 1994 to include 10–13 year olds.

Remands for further police inquiries

Section 60 of the Criminal Justice Act minimises the maximum period a court is able to remand a juvenile, in order for police to make further inquiries into the offence, to 24 hours.

Section 1 of the Criminal Justice and Public Order Act 1994 establishes secure training orders for juveniles aged 12–14 convicted of an imprisonable offence. Secure training orders can be from six months to two years followed by a possible period of supervision. Section 17 has increased the maximum length of detention for juvenile offenders aged 15–17 from 12 months to 24 months.

Detention by the police before court

Section 59 of the Criminal Justice Act 1991 amends s 38 of the Police and Criminal Evidence Act (PACE) 1984 so that a custody officer at a police station must transfer a juvenile offender to local authority accommodation until he appears before the court, unless the custody officer decides:

- that it is impracticable to transfer the juvenile to local authority accommodation; or
- where the juvenile is aged 15 or over, that no secure accommodation is available and that keeping him in other local authority accommodation would not be adequate to protect the public from serious harm.

Bail

When a case is adjourned and a juvenile is remanded the first thing for the court to consider is bail. Under the provisions of the Bail Act 1976, the presumption of the right to bail is greater in the case of a young offender than an adult. If bail is refused, the alternatives available to the court will be determined by the juvenile's age and sex. If the young person is 17 years old (either sex) the juvenile is remanded in custody. If the young offender is under 17, the court can remand him to local authority accommodation. Section 23 of the Criminal Justice and Public Order Act 1994 allows the police to arrest a juvenile who has breached a condition of his remand. Boys under 15 and girls under 17 are prohibited from being remanded in custody. However, s 24 of the Criminal Justice and Public Order Act 1994 allows for the detention of arrested juveniles after charge.

Supervision orders

The Youth Court will be able to grant either a probation order or a supervision order to a 16 or 17 year old. The maximum amount of work that can be imposed in a community service order is 240 hours for offenders aged 16 and 17. Juveniles aged 16 and 17 can be made to attend an attendance centre for up to 36 hours. The new combination order introduced by s 11 of the 1991 Act will be available for 16 and 17 year olds as well as adults.

Rises in youth custody

The public concern over juvenile crime appears to be forcing a backward slide to custodial sentences for young offenders. Statistics provided by the National Association for Care and Resettlement of

Offenders (NACRO) in *Monitoring the Criminal Justice Act in the New Youth Court* show that during the first six months of the Criminal Justice Act 1991 the courts showed restraint in the use of custody and made little use of community sentences previously only for adults. However, as the public mood towards young offenders changes, NACRO points out that these measures will not be sustained. NACRO studied youth courts under the 1991 Act: more than 5% of the 15 to 17 year olds eligible for custody were sent to a young offenders institution. That compares with a national figure of 8% of the 14 to 16 year olds being given custodial sentences under the previous system in 1991. The maximum period for detention of 15–17 year olds was increased to two years in February 1995 (previously one year). In May 1997 the prison population stood at an all time high passing the 60,000 mark. An identified cause of this increase in prison population figures is the number of young persons under 18 sentenced or remanded in custody – almost double since 1993. Concern over repeated offending whilst on bail, the rapid increase in youth crime, and the controversy surrounding the James Bulger case, has stirred the government into moving away from their rehabilitation stance on youth punishment to a policy of sanctioning more custodial sentences for juveniles. The non-interventionist stance in respect of youth crime so prevalent in the early 1990s, where the increased use of cautioning by the police was seen as a viable initiative, has now given way to tougher sentences for juveniles. The Labour government who promise to be 'tough on crime, and tough on the causes of crime' appear set on continuing with legislation to control youth crime. The Criminal Justice and Public Order Act 1994 which introduced secure training centres for 12–14 year olds could be a prelude for the yet to be implemented Crime (Sentences) Act 1997 which would introduce mandatory prison sentences for certain categories of recidivists aged 18 and over.

The Crime and Disorder Bill, announced in the Queen's Speech, could put forward more interesting proposals in respect of controlling youth crime and the notion of fast-tracking juvenile justice. Amongst the proposals is the abolition of repeated cautions in favour of a single final police warning, and scraps the presumption of innocence of 10 to 13 year olds. Curfews for 10 year olds have also been advocated but it is proving difficult in terms of workability. That trend appears to be reversing. NACRO figures demonstrate that from April to September 1993, the custodial sentence figure has risen to nearly 6%. A trend towards harsher sentencing has begun.

Classification of offences and committal proceedings

Classification of offences:

- Indictable offences
  These are the most serious offences. They can only be dealt with at the Crown Court and include offences such as murder, manslaughter, rape, GBH and robbery. These offences are triable only on indictment, triable by both judge and jury in the Crown Court.
- Summary offences
  These are the least serious offences which normally do not result in a custodial sentence. Offences are triable summarily in the magistrates' court.
- Triable either way offences
  These are serious offences eg theft, burglary and assault and can be dealt with either at the magistrates' court or at the Crown Court.

The division between these different categories of offences is not precise; how the offence is defined will usually depend on the form the crime takes, eg whether it is subject to violence, or threats of violence. There is a trend today for magistrates to deal with more and more triable either way offences, and many indictable offences have been reduced to summary level. D Riley and J Vennard in their *Home Office Research Study 98, 1988 Triable Either Way Cases* found that because magistrates have gained a reputation for convicting more defendants than juries, in respect of certain types of cases, the percentage of offences classed as summary has risen. For expediency, if a triable 'either way' offence can be dealt with by the magistrates then it is thought best for them to deal with it; 60% of sentences for 'either way' offences in the Crown Court came within the magistrates jurisdiction. Section 19 of the Magistrates' Courts Act 1980 provides that magistrates need to take into consideration all the circumstances of the case. Recent guidelines by a working party headed by Farquharsen LJ have laid down further criteria regarding 'either way' offences; they are, *inter alia*:

- the level of court the case is to be heard in should not depend on expediency;
- magistrates are to conclude that the prosecution's facts are correct;
- the defendant's antecedents and other circumstances are not to be taken into consideration;
- complicated cases dealing with points of law or fact should be heard in the Crown Court;

- a juvenile defendant, if jointly accused with an adult, should not be committed to the Crown Court for trial unless it is in the public interest.

These guidelines were updated in January 1995, a revised set of guidelines were issued by the Secretariat of the Criminal Justice Consultative Council.

Mode of criminal trial

For a summary offence the defendant pleads guilty or not guilty. If a guilty plea is entered then the court hears the full facts of the offence. When magistrates have obtained sufficient information about the offence and the offender, they will pass sentence. Where the defendant pleads not guilty, the case will be adjourned for trial. Where magistrates decide that a summary trial is most suitable, the defendant, with his consent, will be tried by the magistrates. If the magistrates decide on trial on indictment, or the accused wishes to be tried this way, then committal proceedings will take place before trial. In 1995 79,000 defendants were committed for trial to the Crown Court. Information collected by the CPS shows that 66% of defendants pleaded guilty at the Crown Court.

Committal proceedings

The court is concerned to discover whether there is a case to answer. There are two types of committal proceedings:

- Section 6(1) of the Magistrates' Courts Act 1980 s 6(1) (long form committal)

In the case of 'long committal' proceedings, all prosecution witnesses are examined in the magistrates' court. Prosecution or defence can choose this style of committal proceedings.

- Section 6(2) of the Magistrates' Courts Act 1980 s 6(2) (short form committal)

The majority of committals take place in a few minutes. All the evidence is put before the court in the form of written statements.
Under s 102 of the Magistrates' Courts Act 1980:

- the statement must be signed by its maker; and
- must contain a declaration of truth; and
- there must not be any objection by any of the parties to the state-

ment being produced in evidence. An application for bail can be dealt with at this point as well as questions concerning legal aid for the defendant.

Section 44 of the Criminal Justice and Public Order Act 1994 abolishes the process of a magistrates' court sitting as examining justices. The new 'Transfer to Trial' system will replace committal proceedings. The prosecution serves on the magistrates' court a notice of the prosecutions case. This will detail, *inter alia*, the charges and will contain documents of the evidence on which the charges are founded. The prosecution also serves a copy of the notice on the accused, the court then transfers the proceedings for the trial of the accused to the Crown Court.

Summary trial

A summary trial usually takes place before a bench of three lay magistrates, or a single stipendiary magistrate. The Magistrates' Courts Act 1980 governs the procedure. In some minor motoring offences the defendant may plead guilty by post (s 12 of the Magistrates' Courts Act 1980).

The summary trial commences with the clerk putting the information to the defendant who then has to make a plea of guilty or not guilty. The prosecution opens the proceedings with a summary of the background of the case. The prosecution then offers evidence and produces any witnesses. The defence is allowed to cross-examine the prosecution witnesses to try and discredit their evidence.

Trial on indictment

A trial on indictment is heard in the Crown Court in the presence of a jury. The prosecution opens the proceedings with a speech explaining the process of the trial to the jury. The prosecution outlines the facts and background of the case against the accused. Prosecution then calls witnesses and defence has the right to cross-examine. The defence then puts its case and calls its witnesses. Closing speeches are made by both the prosecution and defence. The judge sums up the case to the jury, explaining, *inter alia*, the standard and burden of proof required, the law, rules of evidence and the need to bring a unanimous decision.

'Cracked' trials

Section 49 of the Criminal Procedure and Investigations Act 1996 has amended the procedure for deciding the mode of trial to help deal with 'cracked' trials (where the defendant reserves his plea for the

Crown Court trial and then pleads guilty at the arraignment). Magistrates will now, by virtue of s 49, be able to make mode of trial decisions with full knowledge of the defendant's intended plea and be able to retain jurisdiction if necessary.

The Royal Commission on Criminal Justice

The great majority of criminal trials are conducted in a manner which all the participants regard as fair, and we see no reason to believe that the great majority of verdicts, whether guilty or not guilty, are not correct ... But the damage done by the minority of cases in which the system is seen to have failed is out of all proportion to their number.

(Report of Royal Commission on Criminal Justice, 1993, Cmnd 2263)

The Royal Commission on Criminal Justice (the Runciman Commission) was set up against a backcloth of a string of miscarriages of justice and a deepening sense of lack of public confidence in the police and our criminal justice system.

Recent events such as the Guildford Four and the re-opening of the Maguire Seven and Birmingham Six cases have sought to undermine confidence in the Court of Appeal. It has been described as 'the institution responsible for upholding, maintaining and sustaining miscarriages of justice' (Gareth Pierce, solicitor representing appellants in the Birmingham Six case, speech to the conference on 'British Criminal Justice in Crisis' 6 July 1990) and, 'an institution with its credibility in tatters' (Stephen Sedley QC, barrister representing appellants in the Carl Bridgewater case, speech to the conference on 'British Criminal Justice in Crisis' 6 July 1990).

Indeed, as the Runciman Committee was sitting, the media drama surrounding the Judith Ward case, Stephan Kiszko and the Cardiff Three was being played out. These miscarriages of justice fuelled the mistrust of the reforms of police practice and procedures put in place by PACE, and of other measures of reform such as the establishing of the Crown Prosecution Service and the duty solicitor scheme, advocated by the Philips Commission.

The terms of reference which the Runciman Commission had to address attracted much criticism. The Commission was:

... to examine the effectiveness of the criminal justice system in England and Wales in securing the conviction of those guilty of criminal offences and the acquittal of those who are innocent, having regard to the efficient use of resources.

(RCCJ p 3)

Specific areas of the system were to be investigated, criminal defence arrangements and access to expert evidence; conduct and supervision of police investigations; the role of experts and forensic evidence; uncorroborated confessions; the role of prosecutors and access to discovery documents to the defence.

The Commission had two years to complete its remit. Special research studies were undertaken. One of these studies by a member of the Commission, Professor Michael Zander, was referred to throughout the report ('The Crown Court Study', 1993) which gathered data on all Crown Court cases dealt with over a two week period in February 1992.

In July 1993 the Royal Commission's report was published detailing 352 recommendations, in the hope of boosting public confidence in the function and fairness of the administration of justice process. There has been much criticism levied at the Royal Commission on Criminal Justice's report, mostly focused on mode of trial, defence disclosure and formalising plea bargaining. Professor Mike McConville of Warwick University expressed concern that 'the balance of the Royal Commission's proposals favour securing convictions rather than safeguarding defendant's rights'.

One of the Commission's proposals is to abolish the right, in 'either way' cases, to elect for trial by jury. The decision in these cases is to rest with magistrates; Michael Zander advocates that this will lead to shorter sentences for convicted offenders. Zander asserts that the proposals were directed towards defendants who elect for Crown Court trial and then plead guilty. However, Professor McConville argues that the consequence will be to deny those individuals who contest eitherway cases through to jury trial, many of whom are subsequently acquitted. McConville argues that because of the serious implications for defendants accused of 'either-way' offences, these defendants should retain the right to a jury trial. He further asserts that there is a difference between defendants who waive the right to a trial by jury after independent advice (90% who are presented with the choice tend to do so); but it is something else completely for the State to take away that right of choice and leave it to magistrates to decide, particularly when the current trend facing magistrates is to retain more cases because of financial restraints.

McConville has been scathing in his comments regarding the Royal Commission's report. He asserts:

It is not empirically grounded; it deploys defective reasoning; it is based on a flawed understanding of the organising principles of criminal justice, and it lacks the intellectual weight and moral authority to support the changes it proposes.

McConville also criticises the Commission's proposals for formalising plea bargaining, whereby the defendant is allowed to ask the judge what the maximum sentence would be if they pleaded guilty at that stage. McConville argues this will pressurise the innocent to plead guilty. Professor Zander argues, however, that the report emphasises that the Commission was aware of the risk of the innocent pleading guilty, but that the risk was created by the sentence discount, and that the Commission's proposals will not increase this risk.

The Police and Magistrates' Courts Act 1994

Increased governmental interference in the police and magistrates' courts service underlies the theme of the Police and Magistrates' Courts Act 1994. The government wants to see more efficiency in the administration of the police and courts. The White Paper which preceded the Bill asserted that the aim of the legislation was to help promote public involvement in the efforts to 'defend the values of our society'. Among the new powers to be given to the Home Secretary is the power to appoint five out of 16 members of police authorities as well as selecting a chairman. The principle of accountability is promoted with fixed term contracts for Chief Constables and the power of the Secretary of State to dismiss them.

Magistrates' courts

New reforms in the constitution of the Magistrates' Courts Committees and the appointment of chief justice's clerks, is giving rise for concern. The Lord Chancellor will now have the duty of appointing the chairman and some members of the Committee (he already appoints magistrates and approves the appointment of clerks). Also, the Lord Chancellor, by statutory instrument, will be able to require that certain features be included in a justice's clerks contract.

The current position

Justice's clerks hold office 'during the pleasure' of the Magistrates' Courts Committee. The Committees consist of magistrates appointed by the local benches. They are funded 80% by central and 20% by local government. Appointment of a justice's clerk is subject to approval by the Lord Chancellor. The clerk can be removed by the Committee after consultation with his benches.

The changes

An Inspectorate has been appointed. This is an integral part of the Lord Chancellor's Department, thus it lacks the independence of government which is necessary if it is not to be viewed as a 'government tool'. Further changes are:

- an extra tier of management (a chief justice's clerk) in each Committee area;
- a reduction in the numbers of Committees from 105 to 50;
- a requirement that the appointment of the Committee's chairman should require the Lord Chancellor's approval;
- provision of default powers entitling the Lord Chancellor to suspend a Committee and to direct a neighbouring Committee to take it over;
- the abolition of the clerk's 'office' and the introduction for both chief justice's clerks and justice's clerks of fixed term contracts of not more than five years with elements of performance related pay;
- the introduction of powers allowing the Lord Chancellor to amend a justice's clerk's contract of employment.

The constitutional issue

It is argued that these proposals will increase ministerial intervention; with the opportunity to interfere with the judicial process. Dicey's 'separation of powers' is threatened. Direct intervention by the government is unacceptable interference in the judiciary; increased efficiency and accountability are all very laudable, but they should not be gained at the cost of more government intervention.

Investigation of crime

Arrest under warrant

A police officer can arrest and detain an individual as part of the process of the enforcement of the criminal law. The normal method of arrest is under a warrant issued by a magistrate or higher judicial officer. Under s 1 of the Magistrates' Courts Act 1980, the police officer lays a written information in oath before a magistrate stating that a person has or is suspected of having committed an offence. The offence must be an indictable offence or a serious offence liable to carry a custodial sentence (Criminal Justice Act 1967).

Before the PACE 1984 was introduced, an arrest was used by the police to bring a suspect before the courts. However, under ss 25 and 27 of PACE 1984, a constable has the power to arrest for other reasons. PACE 1984 sought to rationalise a list of statutory police powers of arrest and the majority are now embodied within the 1984 Act, though there are a number of statutes which contain powers of arrest as well.

Arrests under warrant are in the minority, particularly since the introduction of PACE 1984. Most warrants are issued under the Magistrates' Courts Act 1980 which can be issued against any adult who the police suspect of having, or who has committed, an imprisonable offence, or whose whereabouts are not known. The Magistrates' Courts Act 1980 also provides for bench warrants to be issued against individuals who do not appear in court when they have been served with a summons. Warrants can be issued with the requirement for bail attached, or not, as the case may be.

Arrest without warrant

Under s 24 the police have wide powers to arrest without warrant. Some of these powers of arrest are open to the ordinary citizen. However, when making a 'citizen's arrest', the ordinary person can leave themselves open to a charge of false imprisonment by the individual detained, if the arrest has no real grounds.

Arrest for non-arrestable offences

Only the police have the power to arrest an individual for a non-arrestable offence. This can be done if any of the general arrest conditions under s 23(3) are satisfied, namely:

- the name of the suspect is unknown or cannot be discovered; or
- there are reasonable grounds for believing arrest is necessary in order to protect the suspect from:
  (i)   causing physical injury to himself or some other person; or
  (ii) suffering physical injury; or
  (iii) causing loss or damage to property; or

(iv) committing a public decency offence; or

(v) causing unlawful obstruction of the highway.

In *G v DPP* (1989) G, the appellant, went to a police station with other juveniles to complain that they had been ejected from a bus. The police officer asked the juveniles for their names and addresses, some gave false names and addresses, but G gave his correctly. The officer did not believe G because in his experience people who committed offences did not generally give their real name and address. The juveniles became abusive and G was arrested for 'disorderly behaviour in a police station', and assaulting a police officer in the execution of his duty. It was held because 'disorderly behaviour' was not an arrestable offence, the officer had no power to arrest G. Further, the power the officer did have under s 25(3) was not found to be sufficient ground since the excuse the officer gave about people committing offences giving false details about their name and address was not sufficient since the juveniles had not committed any offences.

Arrestable and serious arrestable offences are defined in ss 24 and 116. Section 24 defines arrestable offences as:

- offences where the sentence is fixed by law, namely murder and treason where only a life sentence may be imposed;
- offences where a person of at least 21 years of age may be sentenced to a term of five years' imprisonment on a first conviction;
- miscellaneous offences under the Customs and Excise Acts;
- offences under the Official Secrets Acts of 1920 and 1989;
- two offences under the Sexual Offences Act 1956;
- two offences under the Theft Act 1968.
- Arrestable offences can also include attempting; conspiring; inciting; aiding; abetting; counselling or procuring any of the above named.

Section 61(1) of the Criminal Justice and Public Order Act 1994 allows a uniformed police officer to arrest a person he suspects is committing an offence under s 61 (trespassers to land). Section 63(8) extends these powers to individuals gathering for a rave.

Powers of arrest (s 24)

Section 24 defines the powers of arrest:

- anyone may summarily arrest (without warrant) any person who is reasonably suspected of committing an arrestable offence or is actually committing such an offence;

- or any person who has committed an arrestable offence or is reasonably suspected to have done so.
- The police may also arrest a person who is about to commit an
  arrestable offence.

Section 24 states:

Where a constable has reasonable grounds for suspecting that an arrestable
offence has been committed, he may arrest without warrant anyone whom he
has reasonable grounds for suspecting to be guilty of the offence.

In *Hussein v Kam* (1970) 'suspicion' was defined as a state of conjecture
where proof is lacking.

In *James v Chief Constable of South Wales Police Force* (1991) an arresting officer had received information concerning a burglary. A police
informant, whom the officer was told was extremely reliable, stated
that the sale of the burglary proceeds was to take place at the house of
the defendant (who was the girlfriend of one of the burglars). She was
arrested, but later released without charge. She claimed damages for
unlawful arrest.

The trial judge ruled that she had been wrongfully arrested because,
inter alia, the arrest was based solely on the word of an informant that
she was going to be involved in the sale of stolen goods, but she had
not yet committed a crime. The Chief Constable appealed.

It was held that it was possible for reasonable suspicion to be based
on information gained from an informant. However, this information
had to be treated with caution; in this the arresting officer had acted
correctly. Further, it is not possible to arrest an individual on the basis
that they were suspected of going to be involved in an offence. But, in
this case, the accused would have handled stolen goods, if she at any
time after the burglary, knowing them to be stolen, or believing them
to be stolen, still received them. The court decided that the arresting
officer had suspected the defendant of having been guilty of handling
stolen goods. His suspicions were reasonable on the existing facts.

In *Chapman v DPP* (1989) an officer, PC Sneller, acting on the instructions of a colleague, tried to gain entry to a flat in order to arrest C's
son for an assault on the first officer. PC Sneller was prevented and
was subjected to physical and verbal abuse by C who denied him
access to the flat. C was charged with assaulting PC Sneller in the execution of his duty. However, there was no evidence that PC Sneller was
aware of the seriousness of the assault on his colleague by C's son. If
there was reason for him to suspect a s 47 offence, he would have had
the power to arrest C's son under s 24 of the PACE 1984, and to gain

entry to the flat in order to do so under s 17(1)(b) of PACE 1984. However, common assault is not an arrestable offence under s 24. It was held that the only relevant power of entry without a warrant would have been if PC Sneller had in fact reasonably suspected C's son to have been guilty of committing an arrestable offence. But there was no evidence to support this. Bingham LJ stated that the omission was fatal to the conviction (see also *Riley v DPP* (1990); *Plowden v DPP* (1991); *Griffiths v DPP* (1991)).

Under s 116 an arrestable offence could become a serious arrestable offence if there is:

- serious harm to state security or public order;
- serious interference with the administration of justice in a particular case;
- serious injury or death, or substantial gain or loss.

Common law arrest for breach of the peace

Under the common law any individual can arrest anyone who is committing a breach of the peace. A constable can arrest anyone who is obstructing him in the execution of his duty and can call upon the general public to assist him, using reasonable force if necessary. There is no need for arrest to be followed by a charge. The person can be released without being able to claim that he has been falsely imprisoned (*Mohammed-Holgate v Duke* (1983)).

The power of the police to enter and deal with a breach of the peace is embodied in a number of cases (*McConnell v Chief Constable of the Greater Manchester Police* (1990); *R v Howell* (1981); *Lamb v DPP* (1989)).

In *McConnell v Chief Constable of the Greater Manchester Police* (1990) McConnell refused to leave a carpet store when he was asked to do so by the manager. When a police officer removed McConnell off the premises, McConnell attempted to enter the store again. McConnell was arrested because of conduct whereby a breach of the peace may be occasioned. McConnell was taken to the magistrates' court to be bound over to keep the peace. However, the magistrates refused and McConnell subsequently sued the police for false imprisonment, arguing a breach of the peace could not occur on private premises. The Court of Appeal rejected his arguments.

Arrest procedures

When a police officer arrests an individual with or without warrant, he must make it clear to the individual that he is being arrested and state the reason for the arrest. If this is not possible then the person being arrested should be informed as soon as is practicable to do so (s 28 of PACE 1984). If these rules are not observed it could render the arrest unlawful. Section 29 of PACE 1984 deals with arrests made while the individual is at the police station voluntarily. Section 30 embodies the general requirement whereby an individual must be taken as soon as possible to a police station after arrest.

The police do not have the power to detain an individual in order that that person helps them with their inquiries. The person must be actually arrested. In *R v Lemsatef* (1977) Lawton LJ stated that:

It must be clearly understood that neither custom officers nor police officers have any right to detain somebody for the purposes of getting them to help with their inquiries.

Section 29 of PACE 1984 states that a person who attends a police station to assist the police in their inquiries has the right to leave at any time, if the police do not arrest him. However, there is no legal duty on the police to point out this fact to an individual and many people believe that the police have a right to insist they help them in their investigation. The protection of a suspect's rights under PACE 1984 does not come into effect until the suspect has been arrested and so it is in the interest of the arresting officer to delay arrest.

On when to arrest, see Ian McKenzie, Rod Morgan and Robert Reiner 'Helping the Police with their Inquiries: the Necessity Principle and Voluntary Attendance at the Police Station' ((1990) *Criminal Law Review*). Though the police are under no duty to inform the suspect of his rights prior to arrest, if it is thought that the delay in arresting the suspect was deliberate in order to circumvent PACE 1984, then a court may exclude any confession that results from the questioning on the ground of either oppression under s 72(2)(A) or unfairness under s 78. This was the case in *R v Ismail* (1990).

Booking in

When a suspect is detained by the police, he must be taken to a designated police station. Section 36 provides that designated police stations should have a custody officer who will normally be the rank of sergeant. It is the custody officer who decides whether to detain the suspect. The custody officer must inform the suspect of the reason for his arrest. The custody officer must then inform the suspect of his rights under PACE 1984. A suspect has the right to have someone informed of his arrest, he has the right to consult a solicitor and to consult the Codes of Practice. Written notice of confirming these rights is given to the suspect. A custody record is opened and the suspect is searched. The custody officer is the guardian of the suspects rights while he is in detention and thus he must remain independent from the investigation. However, this is difficult to sustain, if, for example, while searching the suspect, evidence may come to light of another offence. In *R v Absolam* (1988) the custody officer was aware that the suspect who had been arrested for threatening behaviour also had previous convictions for drugs. When searching the suspect the custody officer demanded the suspect 'put the drugs on the table', the suspect complied, thereby admitting to supplying drugs. It is vital to the workings of PACE 1984 that the custody officer remains independent of the investigation, and be seen as the protector of the suspect's rights under the Act, but this, in practice, is very difficult and can result in problems as *Absolam* illustrates.

Searching the suspect

When the suspect is searched by the custody officer the details of the suspects property are recorded in the custody record, including anything seized when the suspect was arrested. Personal items and clothing are normally retained by the suspect (not money or certain valuables) but the custody officer can retain any items with which he believes the suspect may cause injury to himself or others. A strip search can be carried out if this is necessary, and an intimate body search can also be carried out provided it is authorised by at least a superintendent. Intimate searches for drugs or harmful objects should be undertaken by a doctor or nurse or, if not practicable, an officer of the same sex. Section 117 gives the police the power to use reasonable force to search.

Section 54 of the Criminal Justice and Public Order Act 1994 allows, in certain circumstances, intimate samples to be taken from an individual who is not in police detention.

Detention without charge

The police have good reasons to detain a suspect at the police station without charging him. One of the main reasons is in order to obtain information by questioning the suspect. The rules governing interviewing are contained in the Codes of Practice. Meals, refreshment and rest breaks must be given to the suspect during this period. The Codes of Practice lay down guidelines that the police cannot obtain answers to questions by using tricks or oppression and that vulnerable persons must be accorded certain rights. The custody officer must arrange for an 'appropriate adult' to attend if the suspect being interviewed is a juvenile, blind, mentally handicapped, or unable to read. The suspect can object to the appropriate adult being present.

If the suspect is mentally handicapped and makes a confession with no 'appropriate adult' present, the confession may be excluded. However, if the judge admits the confession he has to give a clear warning to the jury on the danger of convicting the suspect on the basis of the confession (*R v Lamont* (1989)).

Under s 38(6) a custody officer can decide that the local authority's proposed place of detention is not suitable and can keep the juvenile in a police station (*R v Chief Constable of Cambridgeshire ex p M* (1991)). Juveniles are not permitted to share a cell with an adult.

A 17-year-old is not entitled to an appropriate adult and is subject to the same regime as adults in respect to detention after charge. Those under 17 years of age, have provisions made under s 36(6) of PACE 1984 (inserted into the Criminal Justice Act 1991).

Medical treatment

The custody officer must also arrange for medical treatment for a detained person. If a doctor decides that the suspect is not fit to be questioned a further medical examination should be undertaken of the suspect before he is questioned, though failure to obtain a subsequent further examination will not breach the Code in itself (*R v Trussler* (1988)). Failure to observe these principles may result in a confession being inadmissible in evidence, particularly if the suspect is vulnerable to suggestion and he is interviewed without an appropriate adult being present (*R v Everett* (1988); *DPP v Blake* (1989)). Intoxicated suspects should not be interviewed and medical attention should be sought. But this can be waived on the authority of a superintendent if the police suspect that an immediate risk or harm to persons or property is likely if an interview does not take place right away.

Time limits

There are strict time limits on the detention of persons without charge. An arrested person may not be detained without charge for more than 24 hours, unless a serious arrestable offence has been committed. If a serious arrestable offence has been committed a superintendent can extend the period to 36 hours to secure or preserve evidence by continued questioning. Where a serious arrestable offence has been committed and the suspect needs to be held in custody beyond the 36 hour period, the police must bring the suspect before a magistrate to extend the time limit to a maximum of 60 hours. The police can detain a suspect under the Prevention of Terrorism (Temporary Provisions) Act 1989 for 48 hours, this can also be extended.

Under PACE 1984 there must be regular review periods of the detention of suspects whether or not they are charged. If the suspect has not been charged with an offence the first review should be carried out no later than six hours after the period the suspect's detention was first authorised; then subsequently every nine hours. Where the suspect has been charged it is the responsibility of the custody officer to carry out regular reviews.

Grounds for delay

In order to justify delay the ground relied on must be supportable given all the facts. Thus in *R v Alladice* (1988) it was not sufficient ground for delay that an accomplice of the suspect was still at large and might be alerted, because the arrest was made in a public place in front of people known to the suspect. Further, it was not sufficient ground for delay when the suspect's mother had been informed of the arrest by telephone before the decision to delay access to a solicitor had been made (*R v Samuel* (1988)).

Access to a solicitor cannot be denied on the ground that allowing access may prejudice police inquiries. Access to a solicitor is one of the most important safeguards for suspects under s 58 of PACE 1984.

Legal advice in the police station

The role of the lawyer in the police station has been the subject of much recent debate. Very little is known as to the contribution lawyers make at interviews or about whether they in fact offer adequate protection to suspects. Recent research for the Royal Commission on Criminal

Justice by Professor John Baldwin, 'The Role of Legal Representatives at Police Stations' (1993), concludes that, on the whole, solicitors are performing badly at police interviews. They tend to adopt a passive role rather than confront issues on behalf of their client.

In 1986 the Law Society's Criminal Law Committee published a guideline booklet for solicitors advising suspects in the police station. The guidelines asserted, *inter alia*, that the solicitor was not there merely as an observer, and that in order to protect his client a solicitor may have to intervene during the police interview. In *R v Miller* (1992) the Court of Appeal allowed appeals against conviction for murder of the Cardiff Three. Lord Taylor described the interview as a 'travesty' and, referring to the guidelines, said:

It is of the first importance that a solicitor fulfiling the exacting duty of assisting a suspect during interviews should follow the guidelines and discharge his function responsibly and courageously. Otherwise, his presence may actually render dis-service.

Professor Baldwin in his study viewed 400 video recorded interviews and examined 200 audio recordings made during October 1989 and November 1990 in the Midlands and London. He stated that:

- 'lawyers simply do not see it as their function to obstruct the course of police questioning';
- '66.5% of legal representatives say nothing in interviews ... their role is interpreted in practice as an essentially passive one'.

In the light of Professor Baldwin's research the Royal Commission has proposed a revision of the guidelines for solicitors and has advocated better training for solicitors advising clients at police stations.

The Duty Solicitor Arrangements 1990 came into force in April 1990 being the product of the Legal Aid Board's first substantial reassessment of the police station and court duty solicitor schemes since taking over responsibility from the Law Society in April 1989.

The most important changes centre on the duties of the solicitor in responding to a call. Previously, although a duty solicitor on a rota was obliged to accept a call from the regional telephone service, whether he would attend the suspect personally was left to the solicitor. Many solicitors stated that they provided the same service for all clients, whether acting as duty or 'own' solicitor. However, this was not borne out by the study undertaken at Birmingham University, 'Advice and Assistance at Police Stations and the 24-Hour Duty Solicitor Scheme' (1990). This report found that though duty solicitors made less use of representatives than 'own' solicitors, they did give more telephone advice than 'own' solicitors. 'Own' solicitors were twice as likely to attend the police interview as duty solicitors.

The new arrangements attempt to deal with these discrepancies. A duty solicitor on a rota, or a panel duty solicitor who accepts a call, must provide initial advice to suspects who have asked for the duty solicitor, by talking to them directly on the telephone. The only circumstances where initial telephone advice does not have to be given are where:

- the solicitor is already at or near to the police station and can provide advice to the suspect immediately;
- the suspect is not capable of speaking to the solicitor because of intoxication or violent behaviour, in these cases the solicitor must arrange to provide the initial advice as soon as is practicable.

The solicitor must attend the police station when the initial advice is provided, if the suspect requests this; where the suspect has been arrested for an offence under s 24 of the PACE 1984 and the police wish to interview him; or the police intend to hold an identification parade; or the suspect complains of serious maltreatment by the police.

Interviews: conduct and control

In *R v Absolam* (1989) the court stated that:

... there was not in any formal sense a conventional interview ... but equally it was an interview within the provisions of the Code, in that it was a series of questions directed by the police to a suspect, with a view to obtaining admissions on which proceedings could be founded.

In *Absolam* the Court of Appeal quashed the defendant's conviction for supplying cannabis and replaced it with one of possession because the defendant had not been informed of his rights to consult a solicitor before being questioned by the police.

There has been much debate as to what actually constitutes 'an interview', and the Report of the Royal Commission on Criminal Justice (1993) recommends that:

... the definition of an interview in Code C Note for Guidance 11A should be clarified to remove the apparent confusion as to what constitutes an interview for the purposes of the Code.

(para 38)

In *DPP v Rous* (1992) the respondent, who was observed by the police driving her car erratically, was requested to take a breathalyser test.

She refused to do so and was subsequently arrested. When she was at the police station she provided two specimens of breath, the analysis of which entitled her to a statutory blood/urine option, which she declined. The police adhered to the procedure of the MP Book II whereby they recorded their conversation with the defendant with regards to the statutory option. The defendant asserted that those parts of the conversation which entailed questions and answers amounted to an interview, and that paras 11 and 12 of Code C, issued under s 66 of PACE 1984 therefore applied. As she was not given access to the book in order to read it, as required by paras 11 and 12, the magistrates were asked to exercise their discretion under s 78 of PACE 1984 to exclude the evidence regarding the respondent's statutory option. The magistrates found that the questions and answers did in fact amount to an interview and dismissed the information. See further *DPP v D* (1992); *R v Byrne* (1991); *R v Riaz* (1992); *R v Burke* (1992).

In *R v Chung* (1991) the defendant was questioned at his flat after being arrested and after he had been detained at the police station, where he had asked to consult with his solicitor, but was denied access. He was only allowed access to his solicitor after he had confessed. It was held that the questioning before allowing him access to his solicitor (under s 58), the failure to record his admissions immediately, and the failure to show the note to him when it was made, or to inform the solicitor of the existence of the note, rendered the confession unreliable under s 76(2)(b). The evidence was also inadmissible under s 78 (*R v Absolam* (1989)).

In *DPP v Davis* (1991) the statutory procedure under ss 7 and 8 of the Road Traffic Act 1988 with respect to obtaining breathalysers from drivers did not constitute an interview for the purposes of Code C. Evidence was, therefore, wrongly excluded by justices under s 78 of PACE 1984.

In *R v Langiert* (1991) on searching a defendant's premises weapons were found and the police questioned him regarding these. The defendant was convicted of handling stolen goods. He appealed on the ground that his answers to the police questions during the search should have been excluded under s 78. The court held that the questions did amount to an interview and should therefore have been recorded. However, the judge was correct to hold that it was not practicable at that time to do so.

The evidence was correctly admitted, and the police did not go beyond the questions which they had a right to ask in making the decision whether to seize the weapons.

The decision in *DPP v McGladrigan* (1991) is ambiguous. It was held in this case that although s 78 is not confined to cases of *mala fides* on the part of the police, in cases dealing with breathalysers, it could be the deciding element.

Confession evidence and admissibility

The general principles developed by the courts to govern interviews are:

- Suspects must be cautioned before an interview takes place. The caution must make it clear to the suspect that he is not obliged to say anything or answer any police questions (*R v Saunders* (1988)). On every new occasion a suspect is exposed to police questioning he should be given a further caution (*Brown (Kingsley)* (1989)).
- The provisions of PACE must be complied with particularly in respect of meal breaks and rest periods.
- Interviews at police stations must be recorded contemporaneously unless impracticable to do so; a record should be made as soon as possible, and it must be shown why it was impracticable for the officer to have made the record at the appropriate time (*R v Delaney* (1988)).
- The record of the interview must be shown to the suspect if the suspect is still in custody at the completion of the record.
- Methods employed by the police to obtain evidence must not be used in circumstances which may result in the confession being obtained oppressively, or by threats, or bribes.

Doubts about the reliability of police evidence regarding a confession can lead to the exclusion of the confession evidence under ss 78 and 76(2)(b).

Section 78(2)(b) of PACE 1984 provides for mandatory exclusion of confession evidence if it is found to be unreliable, therefore confession evidence must be discarded by a trial judge if it has been gained by threats or bribes, or by any other factor which might cast doubt on the credibility of the statement. Delay in making a record, and not showing it to the suspect for signing, may cause the confession to be unreliable and inadmissible under s 76(2)(b) (*R v Delaney* (1988)). Failure by the police to make a contemporary record, or failure to show it to the suspect can cast doubt on police evidence, that the confession may have been tampered with in some way (*R v Khan (Hassan)* (1990)). Failure by the police to record interviews causes difficulties for the court when allegations are made of 'verballing' a suspect (*R v Keenan*

(1989); also *R v Canale* (1990)). A confession can be inadmissible if it is obtained by 'oppression' under s 76(2)(a). 'Oppression' has been defined in *R v Fulling* (1987) as being more than mere unlawfulness, involving moral wrongdoing by the police. In *R v Emmerson* (1991) the defendant claimed that the confession he made, which was tape recorded by the police, was false. The defendant claimed that he was anxious about his wife and daughter who were asthmatic, and he was intimidated by the police at the time he made the statement. It was held (following *Fulling* (1987)) that the court must apply the ordinary meaning of the word 'oppression' in s 76(2)(9). Therefore, questioning that was 'rude and discourteous' conducted in a raised voice and the use of bad language, giving the impression of 'impatience and irritation', was not considered to amount to oppression.

In *R v Doolan* (1988) the appellant was convicted of robbery. He asserted that confession evidence should have been excluded under s 76(2)(b) because of breaches of the Code of Practice, namely:

- the police failed to caution the appellant before they questioned him (Code of Practice C, Detention Treatment and Questioning (para 10));
- police officers failed to make a contemporaneous record of the interview during which he was alleged to have confessed; and
- the police failed to show to the appellant notes of the interview which were made after the interview (para 11).

The Court of Appeal applied the proviso to s 2 of the Criminal Appeal Act 1968 and upheld the conviction. However, they agreed with the appellants counsel that the confession evidence should have been excluded under s 76(2)(b), because breaches of the Codes of Practice rendered it unreliable.

In *R v Howard Chung* (1992) the appellant was arrested on the suspicion of the theft of motor vehicles. The police also found a quantity of powder in the appellant's possession, believed to be drugs, which led to the police searching the appellant's flat. The search of the appellants flat revealed a number of blank company cheques and blank insurance notes which the police asserted had been stolen, although the defendant was not the thief, but which he had sold on a number of occasions. No contemporaneous record was made by the police of the interview. When notes of the interview were made later by the four police officers at the police station neither the appellant nor the appellant's solicitor were shown a copy.

The Court of Appeal stated that it was 'quite astonishing' that no contemporaneous record had been kept. It held that these breaches of the Code of Practice, together with the fact that the police had delayed the appellant's access to his solicitor, made the confession unreliable, and therefore inadmissible by virtue of s 76(2)(b).

In *R v Crampton* (1991) the defendant was a drug addict and was suffering from withdrawal symptoms. The defendant made a confession 19 hours after his arrest. The police did not consult a doctor as to whether the defendant was fit to be interviewed (although a doctor later supported the police decision to go ahead with the interview). The police stated they would not have interviewed the defendant had they realised he was suffering from withdrawal symptoms. The court held the evidence was correctly admitted. *R v Goldenberg* (1989) was considered. It was doubtful whether the mere holding of an interview during withdrawal was 'anything said or done which was likely in the circumstances existing at the time to render any such statement unreliable', to render it within the meaning of s 76(2)(b). See also *R v Beckford* (1991).

Entrapment

There is no clear authority to determine whether s 78 allows the exclusion of evidence if an offence is instigated by the police acting as agent provocateurs. Evidence of a crime cannot be excluded because the crime was instigated by an agent provocateur (*R v Sand* (1979)) even though the courts have disapproved of these methods (*Brannan v Peek* (1948)); *Browning v Watson (JWH) Rochester* (1953); *R v Birtles* (1969)). However, s 78 could possibly have prompted change. In *R v Gill and Ranuana* (1989) Lord Lane stated:

Nevertheless, we have no doubt that the speeches in *Sang* and the impact of those speeches are matters to be taken into account by a judge when applying provisions of section 78.

In *R v Christou* and *R v Wright* (1992) police officers posed as dishonest jewellers in an undercover operation. The defendants were tricked into selling stolen goods to the police. The evidence obtained in the undercover operation was admissible at their trial. (Not every trick results in unfairness, criteria of unfairness are the same as common law (*R v Sand* (1980)).) Further, the judges exercise of his discretion could only be impugned if it were unreasonable according to *Wednesbury* principles. Regarding the complaint that the undercover police officers should have cautioned the defendants if they clearly suspected them of a crime, the court held that Code C extended beyond the treatment of those in detention, but only where the suspect was vulnerable to abuse or pressure from police officers under unequal terms. In *R v O'Leary* (1988) the Court of Appeal stated that, subject to unreasonableness, the question of whether the evidence should be admitted under s 78 was a matter for decision by the judge in his discretion with which the Court of Appeal would be reluctant to interfere.

In *R v Heaton* (1993) the appellant was convicted of the manslaughter of her baby son. The mother was of low intelligence and she claimed that the appellant had shaken the child violently to quieten him. The mother had stated she had given the baby Calpol, a children's medicine which contained paracetamol. The defence claimed the death of the baby was caused solely by the wrong drug being given to the child. Evidence from the post-mortem found no traces of paracetamol in the child's body, but evidence of promethazine was found in the baby's blood. This was an active ingredient of another drug that the mother kept in the house. Because the appellant's solicitor could not be contacted the appellant had been in custody for 15 hours before he could consult his solicitor. He was interviewed in the presence of his solicitor and the interview was tape-recorded. The defence sought to exclude the evidence of the appellant's interview pursuant to ss 76 and 78 of PACE 1984, and an application was made for a psychiatrist to give evidence. The trial judge would not allow the psychiatrist's evidence and declared the interview should be admitted. On appeal, the appellant argued that the psychiatrist's evidence should have been admitted and that the trial judge should not have allowed the interview because the police had intimidated the appellant during the interview. The appeal was dismissed.

In *R v Williams* (1991) the defendants were charged with violent disorder. They had answered police questions relating to a homicide in the belief they were merely assisting the police with their inquiries. The admissions of their involvement in fighting were excluded under s 78.

In *R v Taylor (Le Roy)* (1991) the defendant was convicted of robbery and the conviction was upheld. Confrontation identification evidence was rightly not excluded under s 78, this was so even when the defendant had been held without charge outside the permitted time limits.

Identification parades

The general principle is that if the suspect wishes for an identification parade to take place it must be done unless it would be impracticable to do so. The police must ensure that the parade is fair and any identification of a suspect that is made must be reliable. If these procedures are breached then the evidence may be excluded under s 78 of PACE 1984.

In *R v Oscar* (1991) a woman saw a man wearing distinctive items of clothing trying to force open a door. The defendant was arrested a few minutes later near the incident. The woman identified the man as the person she had seen, he was wearing the clothing she had described. The man claimed he was jogging. The defendant appealed against his conviction stating that the identification evidence should not have been admitted. The Court of Appeal dismissed the appeal.

In *R v Nagah* (1991) the police charged the appellant with attempted rape. He agreed that an identification parade should take place. He was then released without charge. On leaving the police station, the rape victim identified him from a nearby police car. The appellant argued the evidence of the street identification should be excluded under s 78 because it breached Code D. The judge ruled the evidence was admissible because the appellant was a suspect who was not 'at the police station' therefore paras 2.1–2.10 did not apply. The Court of Appeal stated that if the police decide an identity parade is necessary and the suspect agrees to it, it should take place unless it is not practicable to do so. If the suspect is released because there is not enough evidence to charge him then it is not permissible to bring the complainant outside the police station for a street identification.

In *R v Grannell* (1989) the owner of a house returned to find it being burgled. She saw the driver and made a note of the colour, make and registration number of the car. An identification parade was held but was aborted because of unfairness to the appellant. One month later, the witness identified the defendant in a group identification. She was in a cafeteria at the court and identified him from people passing through the foyer. The defendant appealed against his conviction because the identification had breached Code D. His appeal was dismissed.

Recent research

A research study carried out by Professor John Baldwin, 'Police Interview Techniques: Establishing Truth or Proof?' ((1993) *British Journal of Criminology* p 325), examined techniques used by the police in interviews. He stated that interviews which result in a defendant making a confession are of paramount importance to the police for expediency and efficiency. Professor Baldwin concluded that there was little evidence of oppression used by the police in interviewing suspects, but that police methods of questioning were inadequate and deficient.

The Royal Commission's recommendations

As the Runciman Committee were sitting when evidence of grave miscarriages of justice was emerging, and as, indeed, it had been set up in response to severe criticism of the criminal justice system, it was not surprising that it would make recommendations to improve the system, though some critics have suggested that the Commission did not go far enough to improve the regulations regarding the interrogation of suspects in police custody. Professor John Baldwin observed in 'Power and Police Interviews' (1993) *New Law Journal* that there were very few new ideas in the proposals and that they fall short of providing comprehensive guidelines for the regulation of police questioning of suspects.

The Commission recommended, *inter alia*:

- If the prosecution evidence is deemed unsafe or unsatisfactory, the judge should be able to stop the case.
- If a confession has been made by the suspect away from the police station, the suspect should be presented with it at the beginning of the first tape-recorded interview made at the police station.
- Where confession evidence is involved in a case, a judicial warning should be issued.

Right to silence

A suspect accused of a criminal offence is not obliged to say anything in their own defence, either at the police station or in court, and judges are not allowed to make any comments regarding the defendant remaining silent. There has long been a school of thought that advocates that although accused persons should be able to remain silent, judges, or the prosecution, should be allowed to bring this fact to the attention of juries, who probably would then infer the accused was shielding his guilt. Commentators in favour of these proposals argued that since PACE 1984 and the safeguards it implemented for a suspect in police custody (access to a solicitor etc), this has considerably reduced the likelihood of confessions being obtained unfairly. Senior police officers argue that if a person is innocent they will want to establish this and that it is only the guilty who remain silent. However, many commentators are very sceptical about these arguments. The safeguards for the suspect embodied in PACE are by no means foolproof. Tape recording of interviews is an important step forward but this does not guarantee that suspects will not be coerced into making statements before the tape-recording process is activated.

It is argued that confessions do not play as crucial a role in the detection of crime as is thought by many people. Professor Michael Zander in his study 'Investigation of Crime' (1979) argues this point. However, confessions may disclose other offences and they can save the investigating officer a lot of work.

Criminal Evidence (Northern Ireland) Order 1988

The Criminal Evidence (NI) Order was enacted in 1988. The justification was that it would be valuable in dealing with 'terrorist' suspects refusing to answer questions in police custody. The Order applies to all criminal suspects.

The order contains four specific restrictions on the right to silence:

- Article 3
  This is specifically to deal with 'ambush' defences. It allows a court or jury to draw adverse inferences if the accused does not mention any fact relied on in his defence when being questioned by police, or being charged, if it was thought reasonable that it should have been mentioned.
- Article 4
  This allows a court or jury to make inferences that appear proper to do so from unanswered questions. The prosecution as well as the judge can comment on an accused's silence. Further, before defence evidence is called the judge must warn the accused, in the presence of the jury, that inferences could be drawn if he refuses to testify.
- Article 5
  Allows a court or jury to make inferences about the accused's failure to explain the presence of objects, substances or marks on his person or clothing.
- Article 6
  Allows inferences to be made regarding a suspect's failure to explain his presence at an offence which he has been arrested in connection with, if the police have reason to suspect that his presence can be linked to the offence.

The Articles allow the court or jury to take the accused's silence as amounting to a possible corroboration of any adverse evidence against the accused. There are no guidelines in the Order to explain what type of inferences can be drawn, though it does prohibit a person being convicted only on an inference which is drawn from the accused's silence.

The Royal Commission (right to silence)

The Runciman Royal Commission on Criminal Justice considered the question of the right to silence and debated whether to accept a practice similar to that in Northern Ireland, or to retain the right to silence, which was proposed by the Philips Royal Commission on Criminal Procedure (1981). The Law Society, the Bar Council and the Magistrates' Association were supportive to the view of retaining the right. The Police, Crown Prosecution Service and HM Council of Circuit Judges were not in favour of retaining the right to silence. The Runciman Royal Commission in its report (1993) recommended in favour of retaining the right to silence. Many commentators argue removing the right will interfere with the defendant's privilege against self-incrimination. Article 6 of the European Convention (fair trial provision) does not actually embody this principle but the European Court in *Funke v France* has proposed that it does come within it.

Despite all the arguments this right was taken away by the Criminal Justice and Public Order Act 1994. Sections 34–39 allow the courts to draw 'such inferences as appear proper' if the accused fails to mention when questioned any fact that he may later rely on as evidence in court.

Bail

The question of bail can arise twice, firstly at the police station and again when the accused has to appear before a court. When bail is granted, it means that a person who is suspected or accused of a crime is released from detention until his case is heard. Bail is defined as the release of a person subject to a duty to surrender to custody at a particular time and place.

Studies have shown that suspects remanded in custody awaiting trial are more likely to plead guilty, be convicted and to be given a custodial sentence, than others released on bail. If a person has been arrested by warrant, the warrant will have provisions included as to whether bail should be granted; this decision is made by the magistrate who issues the warrant. If arrest is not under warrant the police must act in accordance with the provisions contained in PACE 1984. Under PACE 1984 the custody officer is responsible for deciding whether to continue the detention of a suspect who has not been charged. The custody officer will be able to do this if he thinks it is necessary in order to 'secure or preserve evidence relating to an offence for which he is under arrest or to obtain such evidence by questioning him'. A person who has been charged must be released unless:

- the police cannot discover the persons name and address or believe that the information given is false;
- the police reasonably believe that detention is necessary for the persons protection or to prevent the person causing harm to someone else or interfering with property; or
- the police reasonably believe that the person will 'jump bail', interfere with witnesses or otherwise obstruct the course of justice.

A juvenile can be detained in custody 'in his own interests'. Any person who is detained in custody must be brought before a magistrates' court as soon as is practicable. Criminal statistics indicate that there is a large percentage of people granted bail by the police following an arrest. In 1986 the figure was approximately 90%.

Bail from court

The granting of bail from court is governed by the Bail Act 1976. This legislation was passed in response to the wide discretion that magistrates previously had to grant bail and in order to increase the number of defendants released on bail before trial.

Right to bail

Section 4 of the Bail Act 1976 governs the accused's right to bail. However, this section does not relate to all stages in the proceedings. Section 4 gives a right to bail in those cases which do not come within Schedule 1 of the Bail Act 1976. It would be up to the defence in those cases to plead for bail; there is no statutory right in favour of it.

The exceptions to bail are classed in two lists. The first list will apply if the defendant is charged with an offence which carries a possible custodial sentence; the second list applies if the offence is one which does not carry a custodial sentence. If it is an imprisonable offence, a court does not have to grant bail if it believes that the defendant may:

- fail to surrender to custody; or
- commit an offence while on bail; or
- interfere with witnesses or otherwise obstruct the course of justice.

An accused person who is charged with an imprisonable offence may also be refused bail if the court requires reports to be made concerning the accused and deems it fit that he remains in custody while these reports are being compiled. Bail can also be refused if the defendant has previously failed to surrender to the court/police, and there is a possibility this will occur again. If a court grants bail they can also impose conditions on the defendant, eg reporting at regular intervals to a police station, residing at a stated address, or surrendering a passport. The court can still require a 'surety' – a person who will agree to pay the court a sum of money if the defendant fails to appear. If a defendant is refused bail, he must be informed of the reasons why this decision was made. If the accused is not legally represented and bail is not granted the defendant must be informed of his right to appeal to a higher court.

Appeal against refusal to grant bail

If an accused person is not granted bail a record must be made of the reasons why and the defendant can, if he so wishes, obtain a copy. An accused person can appeal against a magistrate's decision not to grant bail to the High Court. The High Court has the power to grant bail or vary any of the conditions attached by magistrates (s 22 of the Criminal Justice Act 1967). An accused person not granted bail can also appeal to the Crown Court which can grant bail if:

- the magistrates have remanded the defendant in custody after a full bail application has been made;
- if the magistrates have committed the defendant to the Crown Court for trial or sentence; or
- if the magistrates have convicted the accused and refused him bail pending appeal to the Crown Court.

The Bail (Amendment) Act 1993 allows the prosecution an appeal to the Crown Court to prevent bail being granted if the accused is charged with certain serious offences.

Reform

There has been much public concern about the number of offences committed by persons who are released on bail, so called, 'bail bandits', and the government is in the process of reforming bail procedures. There is now to be an automatic refusal of bail in homicide cases and in cases of rape or attempted rape, where the defendant has been convicted of a similar offence previously and was given a custodial sentence. Further, if the defendant is already on bail and is charged with an indictable offence, or triable either way offence, the right to bail will be refused (ss 25–30 of the Criminal Justice and Public Order Act 1994). Further, s 5B of the Bail Act 1976 allows the court to reconsider the grant of bail to a defendant if subsequent information is put forward to the court which was not available at the time of granting the bail.

Stop and search

The police powers regarding search of an individual are contained in PACE 1984 and the Home Office Codes of Practice. Under s 1 of PACE 1984 a police officer can stop, detain and search any person that he reasonably suspects may be carrying stolen or prohibited items. Items would include such things as offensive weapons, and articles made or adapted for use in connection with an offence, such as burglary, theft, taking of a motor vehicle, or obtaining property by deception. Section 60 of the Criminal Justice and Public Order Act 1994 allows uniformed officers to stop and search pedestrians, vehicles and their drivers for offensive weapons.

Reasonable grounds for suspicion

This is clarified in the Codes of Practice as being an objective or tangible cause for suspicion on the part of the police officer. The power to stop and search should never be used to establish grounds for a search. The powers must not be used subjectively; individuals should not be stopped and searched by police officers because of the person's race or appearance, or because they are a member of a particular group or community.

PACE 1984 concentrates the main powers of the police in respect of stop and search but there are other statutes which existed before and after PACE which allow the police this power:

- Misuse of Drugs Act 1971
- Firearms Act 1968
- Customs and Excise Management Act 1979
- Aviation Security Act 1982
- Crossbows Act 1987
- Prevention of Terrorism (Temporary Provisions) Act 1989

The Codes of Practice require that when a person is stopped by a police officer, the suspect should be allowed the opportunity to voluntarily hand over the prohibited article; if the suspect objects then the police officer should exercise his powers under s 1 of PACE 1984.

In April 1995 a new edition of the Codes came into force which takes account of the Royal Commission's recommendations and the implemented changes under the Criminal Justice and Public Order Act 1994, s 60. For example, there are new provisions covering stop and search in Code A which deal with the prospect of violence whilst searching, and searches connected with the prevention of terrorism.

Safeguards under s 2 of PACE 1984

Section 2 of PACE 1984 provides the suspect with some safeguards. Under s 2 a police officer who wishes to carry out a stop and search must:

- State their name, their police station and indicate the reason for the search.
- If the officer is in plain clothes he must provide the suspect with written evidence that he is a police officer.
- Section 3 states that a police officer must make a written record of the search immediately or, if this is not practicable, as soon as possible.
- A copy of a search record must be available to the suspect for up to 12 months.
- If a search is made of an unattended vehicle the police officer should leave a notice with his name, police station, and information explaining why the vehicle has been searched.

Section 2 indicates the extent to which a police officer can search a suspect in a public place. This must be confined to outer clothing only. This excludes hats or shoes. If a further search is necessary it should be conducted in a private place. A strip search can only be conducted in a police station. Under s 117 a police officer can use reasonable force in the exercise of his powers.

Under s 163 of the Road Traffic Act 1988 a police officer has the power to stop any motor vehicle. Section 4 of PACE 1984 empowers the police to set up road blocks if a serious arrestable offence has been committed.

Entry search and seizure

Premises under PACE 1984 include: buildings, vehicles, caravans, tents, houseboats, aircraft, etc.

Entry and search by warrant

Section 8 of PACE 1984 provides for a general power for magistrates to issue search warrants to the police where there are reasonable grounds for believing that a 'serious arrestable offence' has been committed eg offences such as murder, manslaughter, rape, etc. The police must have reasonable grounds to suspect that admissible evidence in connection with the offence will be found on the premises and that:

- it is not reasonably practicable to contact any person who could give permission to enter the premises;
- such a person has unreasonably refused to allow the police to enter the premises or hand over the evidence;
- evidence would be hidden, removed or destroyed if the police sought access without a warrant.

There are certain articles which cannot be seized under a warrant such as articles which are subject to legal privilege (ie between solicitor and client). Excluded material includes personal records such as medical records, specimens for medical purposes and certain journalistic material held in confidence.

In *R v Central Criminal Court ex p AJD Holdings* (1992) the court stressed that, when police officers request a warrant they should be clear what evidence it is hoped a search will reveal; further, the application should make it clear how the material they want to seize relates to the crime which is under investigation.

In *R v Billericay Justices and Dobbyn ex p Harris Coaches* (1991) a police officer had the power to require the production of documents in pursuance of s 99 of the Transport Act 1968. The Divisional Court refused the application for judicial review of the magistrates' decision to issue a search warrant.

Section 62 of the Criminal Justice and Public Order Act 1994 states that where trespassers, with vehicles, on land, have been ordered to vacate the land by the police and refuse to do so, the police can seize and retain the vehicles. Sections 63 and 64 give similar powers of seizure of equipment from people intending to hold a rave.

Entry and search without a warrant

Section 18 of PACE 1984 provides the police with the power to enter and search:

> ... any premises occupied or controlled by a person who is under arrest for an arrestable offence, if he has reasonable grounds for suspecting that there is on the premises evidence other than items subject to legal privilege that relates (i) to the offence; or (ii) to some other arrestable offence which is connected with or similar to that offence.

These provisions relate to entry and search after the arrest of a person for an arrestable offence who occupies or controls the premises so that further evidence connected with the offence may be obtained. Section 32 allows the police to enter and search any premises if a suspect is arrested away from the police station and was at these premises on or prior to the arrest, in order to search for evidence of the offence committed.

Where evidence of entry and search after arrest is admitted, it is a question for the jury, not the judge, whether the actual purpose of the police officers search was to search for such evidence. In *R v Beckford* (1991) confirmation was given by the Court of Appeal that, under s 32, the police can enter and search premises if the defendant had been in those premises shortly before arrest. The officers' credibility in respect of the search could be tested by the reasons given for the search.

Delay in exercising suspects' rights

When a suspect has been arrested and is being detained in a police station, he has the right to have a friend or relative informed of his arrest as soon as practicable. However, an officer of the rank of superintendent (or acting rank *R v Alladice* (1988)) can delay the exercise of these rights under s 56(1) of PACE 1984 if:

- the person is detained for a serious arrestable offence;
- an officer of at least the rank of superintendent authorises it; or
- if the officer has reasonable ground to suspect that exercising the right would lead to interference with or harm to evidence connected with a serious arrestable offence or interference with, or physical injury to other persons; or
- will hinder the recovery of any property obtained as a result of such an offence.

If delay is authorised the suspect must be informed of this course of action and it must be recorded in the custody record. When the delay has come to an end the detained person must be informed of this fact. Delay without sufficient good reason could result in the reliability of any confession made during the delay being questioned and rendered inadmissible under s 76(2)(b) or could even lead to exclusion under s 78 because of unfairness (*R v Walsh* (1989); *R v Cochrane* (1988)).

5 The civil process

You should be familiar with the following areas:

- civil court structure
- organisation of civil courts
- Civil Justice Review 1988
- recommendations and implementation
- the civil procedure
- the High Court and the county court

The civil court structure

Key differences between criminal and civil law

Public law includes criminal law, constitutional and administrative law and is concerned with the interaction between an individual and the rest of the community.

Private law includes tests contract and divorce law and concerns the interaction between individuals in that community, in as much as they do not concern the community as a whole. It is possible to be both liable in public and private law.

Criminal law is concerned with conduct which the State disapproves of and will punish the perpetrator, and seek to deter others from similar conduct. Civil law has a complementary function. When a dispute arises between two individuals rules of civil law are applied to determine which individual is in the right. The party in the wrong must then compensate the other for any loss or damage arising. The object of the criminal law is therefore punitive; the object of the civil law is to compensate the person wronged.

There are separate systems of courts to deal with criminal and civil cases.

In England a criminal prosecution is usually brought by the Crown Prosecution Service. This was established by s 1 of the Crown

Prosecution Act 1985. The Director of Public Prosecutions is in charge and can take up any prosecution started by a private individual. The Crown Prosecution Service works independently from the police, and it is they, not the police, which take the decision whether to prosecute. Private individuals can, if they wish, institute a prosecution if they feel the police are not dealing with the matter sufficiently (s 6 of the Prosecution of Offences Act 1985).

A prosecution can be started by laying an information – either written or oral, or by charging an individual for an offence and is usually undertaken by the police in serious offences; the offence is contained in a charge sheet.

Civil and criminal cases are processed differently and different terms are used. In the civil court the person bringing the action is known as the plaintiff. In the civil court the person charged will be known as the defendant or accused. In criminal cases we talk about a prosecution; in civil cases we refer to bringing an action or suing. The language associated with the criminal process is punitive in style.

The magistrates' court

Magistrates are involved with a large number of civil cases dealing particularly with the family. Lay magistrates are specially chosen to sit on panels dealing with family matters. They deal with matters such as judicial separation, maintenance payments, affiliation orders, guardianship of minors, adoptions, care orders etc. They have many administrative tasks such as the issuing and renewing of licences, dealing with community charge enforcement. The Children Act 1989 has widened the powers of magistrates giving them more jurisdiction in respect of child law (in such cases the court is referred to as a 'family proceedings court') and jurisdiction under the new youth court dealing with juveniles under 17 years of age.

In 1997 there were 30,374 unpaid lay magistrates in England and Wales. A total of 89 full-time stipendiary magistrates and 98 acting stipendiary magistrates.

County courts

The county courts were established in 1846 to provide efficient and cheap local justice for various types of civil matters. There are 274 county courts staffed by circuit judges and district judges. Circuit judges must be barristers of at least 10 years' standing, they are appointed by the Crown. They normally sit alone but on occasions (particularly complex fraud cases) a jury of eight can be called. Circuit judges are aided by district judges, who have at least seven years experience of advocacy qualification (s 71 of the Courts and Legal Services Act 1990); they are appointed by the Lord Chancellor. The county courts deal entirely with civil matters.

In 1997 there were 557 circuit judges, 332 district judges, 913 recorders and 348 assistant recorders in England and Wales.

Jurisdiction

The jurisdiction of the county court is governed by the County Courts Act 1984; the Courts and Legal Services Act 1990; the High Court and County Courts Jurisdiction Order 1991 and the County Court Rules 1981. County courts can grant the same remedies as the High Court, except for the prerogative orders of *mandamus, certiorari* and prohibition. Also Anton Piller Orders and Mareva Injunctions. Since April 1995 the responsibility for the administration of the county courts has been that of the Court Services Agency under a chief executive, while wider policy issues remain with the Lord Chancellor's Office. The Court Service Agency is responsible for the implementation of the Courts Charter laying down specific criteria regarding standards and performance related issues. The County Court Practice, published each year, (referred to as the 'Green Book') contains the County Courts Act 1984 and the County Court Rules. Section 75(3) of the County Courts Act 1984 (read with the amended Orders made by the Civil Justice Review) details which jurisdiction and powers of the district judge may be exercised by some other officer. There is a great emphasis on 'revolution', that is for functions such as variation of Orders, suspension of warrants, and Consent Orders to be dealt with primarily by county court staff. These Codes of Practice (or Guidelines) have legal effect as stated by the Master of the Rolls in *Langley v North West Water Authority* (1991): 'Every court has inherent jurisdiction to regulate its own procedures insofar as they were not inconsistent with the statutory rules.'

Types of action

Actions in contract and tort (defamation is heard in the High Court). Personal injuries actions must start in the county court unless there is a possibility the plaintiff will recover more than £25,000 in damages. Where the sum exceeds £25,000 the action will be heard in the High Court, unless the High Court transfers the case to the county court, or if the action is started in the county court and the county court wishes to retain the case. Regard must be had to the criteria laid down in the 'jurisdiction order':

- the true value of the claim including the value of any counter-claim;
- the general importance of the case;
- how complex the case is with regard to the facts – procedures;
- how quickly the case can be dealt with.

Other actions include actions for the recovery of land where the value is not more than £30,000; actions in equity not exceeding £30,000; bankruptcies; winding up of companies; probate proceedings not exceeding £30,000; family matters; consumer credit; landlord and tenant; and patents (under the Copyright, Designs and Patents Act 1988).

By far the largest number of cases handled by the county courts relate to debt recovery. The courts deal with more than 3 million debt claims each year. These are known as default summonses which are different from other types of cases in that no hearing is arranged unless the claim is disputed. The district judge tries cases where the amount is less than £5,000. If it is more than £5,000 or is a case of particular importance it must be heard by a circuit judge. The small claims procedure is a low-cast method of settling small debts without having to use a solicitor. They are mostly concerned with, for example, goods and services supplied which have not been paid for, or minor damage to property.

The small claims procedure is important because it is at this level that most members of the public have contact with the civil justice system. Judicial statistics for 1995 state that county courts tried 24,477 actions, but there were 88,170 arbitration awards. Small claims took 78% of final orders after trial in county courts and 76% in all courts. January 1996 saw the small claims, automatic reference limit increased to £3,000 (except for personal injury claims former limit £1,000 retained). 1995 judicial statistics show that 45% of county court trials ended in a judgment for less than £3,000. In 1996 four out of five civil claims will have been decided by small claims procedures. Lord Woolf has put forward recommendations for increasing the limit to £5,000 which will be welcomed by litigants who see the system as an accessible and important part of our civil justice system.

The High Court

The High Court consists of the Lord Chancellor; the Lord Chief Justice; the President of the Family Division; the Vice Chancellor and puisne judges, ie junior or lower in rank as compared with the Lord Chief Justices of Appeal and other senior members of the judiciary. The High Court is split into three basic divisions, each of which is further divided. In theory, any puisne judge can deal with any High Court matter;

in practice they tend to specialise. Often this specialism reflects their expertise when they were barristers. Each of the three divisions has an appellate jurisdiction. The work is mostly done in separate courts, known as Divisional Courts.

The Chancery Division

First instance jurisdiction entailing administration of estates, mortgages, trusts, rectification of deeds, partnerships, winding-up of companies, bankruptcy, revenue, planning and landlord and tenant disputes. On occasions other cases are dealt with in this division by either courts, for example, the Companies Court, the Patents Court, and the Court of Protection which deals with managing the affairs of mental patients. The courts appellate jurisdiction hears appeals from decisions of the Inland Revenue Commissioners, and appeals on bankruptcy and land registration cases from the county courts. The division is presided over by the Lord Chancellor, but the Vice-Chancellor is responsible for the day-to-day running of the court.

The Family Division

This division was created by the Administration of Justice Act 1970. First instance jurisdiction covers family matters, such as all cases concerning marriage including its validity and termination, legitimacy, hardship, adoption, guardianship and family property disputes and all issues concerning proceedings under the Domestic Violence and Matrimonial Proceedings Act 1976; and s 30 of the Human Fertilisation and Embryology Act 1990. Cases on appeal from the county, magistrates' courts and Crown Courts are dealt with by a Divisional Court of two High Court Judges. The Division is presided over by the President of the Family Division.

The Queen's Bench Division

This is the largest and busiest of the three. It is presided over by the Lord Chief Justice. First instance jurisdiction consists of mainly contract and tort actions. The division also includes the Admiralty Court, which deals with claims for injury or loss through collisions at sea, ownership and loss from ship and salvage. Also included here is the Commercial Court which provides hearings of commercial claims, and an arbitration service for businessmen: claims include, *inter alia*, insurance, banking, agency and negotiable instruments.

The appellate jurisdiction is complex. A single judge can hear appeals from certain tribunals (eg the Pensions Appeals Tribunal) and from commercial arbitrations, particularly on points of law. The Divisional Court, made up of two judges, has a certain civil appeal function, for example, from the Solicitor's Disciplinary Tribunal. It also has two other important functions: it hears appeals from magistrates' courts, which have been to the Crown Court for appeal or sentence, by way of a 'case stated' and further, it exercises the supervisory jurisdiction inherited from the old Court of King's Bench. It oversees the activities of all the inferior courts and can issue the following types of prerogative orders.

- *mandamus*
- prohibition
- *certiorari*
- *habeas corpus*

The House of Lords

The House of Lords is the supreme court of appeal for civil cases in Great Britain and Northern Ireland. An appeal to the House of Lords needs the permission of the Court of Appeal or in certain cases from the High Court or Divisional Court for a leap-frog appeal under the provisions of the Administration of Justice Act. The House of Lords can itself give leave for an appeal where the lower court has refused permission, the procedure being by way of a petition by the Appeal Committee. Appeals to the House are generally only permitted where it is certified that there is some point of law of general public importance that the case merits the consideration of the House of Lords. Appeals are usually heard by one of the two Appellate Committees which normally consist of five Lords of Appeal in Ordinary, generally known as Law Lords. The appeal Committees consist of three Law Lord who report their recommendations to the Appellate Committee. The procedure is relatively informal. At the conclusion of the hearing before the Appellate committee, the Law Lords reserve their judgment, and will then provide written opinions.

Judicial Committee of the Privy Council

This dates back to 1833. It can hear appeals from Ecclesiastical Courts and certain professional tribunals. It hears appeals from the Isle of Man and the Channel Islands and from Commonwealth countries. The members of the committee are:

- The Lord Chancellor
- Lords of Appeal in Ordinary

- Privy Councillors
- Senior Commonwealth Judges

European Court of Justice

Where a point in any case is concerned with the interpretation of community law the final court of appeal in a Member State must refer the case to the European Court for a ruling (Article 177 of the EEC Treaty). The national court must then decide the case in the light of the interpretation dictated to it. If a trial judge decides to interpret the treaty himself, he must do so according to the principles laid down by the European Court (European Communities Act 1972). In England on questions of interpretation or validity, the European Court is supreme. Lord Denning in *HP Bulmer Ltd v J Bollinger SM* (1974) explained the relationship of the European Court to the English system of courts:

The first fundamental point is that the Treaty concerns only those matters which have a European element, that is to say, matters which affect people or property in the nine countries of the Common Market besides ourselves. The Treaty does not touch any of the matters which concern solely England and the people in it, these are still governed by English Law. They are not affected by the Treaty, but when we come to matters with a European element the Treaty is like an incoming tide. It flows unto the estuaries and up the rivers. It cannot be held back, Parliament has decreed that the Treaty is henceforward to be part of our law. It is equal in force to any statute ... any rights or obligations created by the Treaty are to be given legal effect in England without more ado.

Proceedings can be taken against Member States either by the Commission or by another Member State in respect of violations of the Treaties or community legislation.

Organisation of civil courts

There have been many changes in the organisation of civil courts. Changes in the rules governing the civil courts have been of a substantial nature following the recommendations of the Civil Justice Review which was initiated in 1985 to speed up the process and improve access to justice. Lord Mackay summed up the position in 'Litigation in the 1990s' (1991) *Modern Law Review*:

Too many cases of relatively low importance, substance and complexity were being handled and tried at an inappropriately high level. This was wasteful of High Court resources, inflated the costs of smaller cases and clogged up the courts, exacerbating delays.

The Civil Justice Review was concerned to meet the public's criticisms that justice was too slow, inaccessible, very expensive, and extremely complex in its process. In the General Issues paper published in 1987 the concept of 'high quality justice' was emphasised as the fundamental objective in all areas of the civil process.

The High Court, traditionally the centre of all personal injury claims, has been completely reorganised by the Courts and Legal Services Act 1990 (High Court and County Courts Jurisdiction Order 1991).

Reform of civil litigation

In February 1985, the then Lord Chancellor, Lord Hailsham began a review into the machinery of civil justice. The review was undertaken by the Lord Chancellor's Department under the supervision of an advisory committee chaired by Sir Maurice Hodgson. The review centred on five consultative papers concerning civil litigation:

- personal injury
- small claims
- Commercial Court
- debt enforcement
- housing

The final report was published in 1988. Its findings were implemented by the Courts and Legal Services Act 1990.

Principle recommendations

The principle recommendations of the Civil Justice Review were:

- The High Court and county court will remain separate, but the former will deal with public law cases, complex and specialist cases and it will not handle other cases where the amount in issue is less than £25,000. Cases involving between £25,000 and £50,000 could be tried either in the county court or in the High Court.
- All personal injuries cases to start in the county court.
- A new upper tier of circuit judges to be created to deal with the more difficult civil cases while the general trial jurisdiction of county court registrars should be raised to £5,000. Barristers should be eligible for appointment as registrars who should be called judges.
- The same remedies should be available in the county court and the High Court.

- The maximum time for delay after issue of a writ should be reduced from one year to four months and pretrial reviews of High Court cases should be conducted in experimental cases.
- Court staff should undergo more training. There should be more use made of technology, computers and there should be more in-depth training of judges by the Judicial Studies Board. The long vacation for the High Court should be cut from September and August to August only, although judges of the High Court should still only sit 188 days a year.
- The small claims jurisdiction in the county court should be increased to £1,000; the hearings are to be informal, in private and simplified.
- Litigants in small claims, housing or debt cases in the county court ought to have a statutory right to be aided by a lay person of their choice. Court forms and leaflets should be more straightforward, advice agencies should be encouraged to have duty representatives and an experimental scheme of evening arbitration should be con-ducted at a small number of centres.
- In personal injury cases the Lord Chancellor should consider a sys-tem of no fault compensation for less serious road accidents to be financed by personal insurance.
- Simplified procedures to be introduced regarding housing cases and more training for judges in housing work, rent assessment pan-els should be integrated into the national structure of courts and tri-bunals should be administered by the Lord Chancellor.
- The waiting time in the Commercial Court should be reduced to 12 months from the date the trial was set.
- There should be an inquiry commissioned by the Lord Chancellor to examine the housing evidence rule.

Further provisions and amendments are contained in the County Courts (Amendment No 3) Rules 1990. It is felt that openness and dis-closure will develop a more consistent system leading to more settle-ments, enabling the judge to come prepared to the trial with more knowledge of the issues at hand than previously.

- A discretionary power can now be used to enable the exchange of statements of witnesses. This will provide more disclosure between the parties, reducing trial time, because the statements can stand as evidence in chief. The witness cannot then add anything to the evi-dential issues not already contained in his statement.
- Cost penalties will be issued for failure to admit facts or documents already proved.
- Split trials can be ordered.

- A procedure whereby provisional damages can be made to the plaintiff if his medical condition is liable to deteriorate after settlement of the claim.
- In personal injuries claims, both a medical report and a separate statement of special changes calculations with the particulars of claim must be filed.
- The summons must be served within four months of the date of the summons.
- Automatic directions have been extended to assist default and fixed date actions in the county court.

There has been criticism regarding the controversial redistribution of court business. The Civil Justice Review had concluded that too many personal injury cases were going through the High Court. These cases were in fact very straightforward, and there was no need to take up valuable High Court time. Only 36% of awards at trial and 14% of settlements in the High Court were for sums exceeding £20,000. The biggest problem was the time delay in the High Court; litigants waiting up to five years or more. The system was very ponderous and wasteful. The High Court was to be reserved for public law and specialist cases.

Stephen Sedley QC in 'Improving Civil Justice' (1990) *Civil Justice Quarterly* p 348 states that:

It is apparently taken for granted among the judiciary and in the Lord Chancellor's Department that because there are finite judicial resources in the High Court, significant classes of cases have got to be removed from the jurisdiction in order to clear the way for more important litigation. This is not necessarily true, but no adequate research or resources have been put into the exploration of a more efficient but unified system.

Sedley argues (p 348) that these measures were to allow for a 'judicial fast-track' for public law, particularly commercial cases:

... it is clear that a policy choice has been made to prioritise commercial law and public law at the expense of issues arising from things like accidents at work or on the roads, wrongful arrests, contracts of employment or tenancies and housing conditions – in other words, individual's problems.

The increased case-load of personal injuries to the county court have come at a time when the county courts are struggling to cope with the surge in re-possession of houses, mortgage arrears and rent, and many more debt related cases. The new procedures were implemented to cure defects and delays but only appear to have exacerbated them further down the line; despite the assurances from Lord Mackay that the county courts have been made more efficient and are prepared for the task. Solicitors dealing with personal injuries claims have expressed doubts as to whether county court judges are sufficiently trained to deal with the complex evidence involved in these cases. They also express concern that levels of damages awarded in the county courts will be very much lower than previously in the High Court.

Stephen Sedley (p 349) further comments that:

The inevitable corollary of this process in the present hierarchy of courts and tribunals is that individual claims and rights are marginalised and trivialised. The Lord Chancellor's Department allocates them to courts of often poorer quality, and the appellate courts keep them there by placing jurisprudential blocks on the issues that they throw up.

The civil procedure

The High Court

An action in the High Court can be started by:
- An originating summons: normally used in the Chancery Division, it brings before the court the questions to be decided by the court.
- Originating motions: also used by the Chancery Division, normally the application is made orally to the court and written notice is given to the parties concerned in the case.
- Writ of summons: this is normally used in actions in tort for a personal injuries act. The writ notifies the defendant that an action has been originated against him and that he must acknowledge this notification to the court. Usually the writ will take the form of:
  - parties' names;
  - status;
  - the division of the High Court in which the action is to be heard;
  - the claim;
  - the remedy required;
  - information regarding the substance of the action against the defendant;
  - name and address of the plaintiff's solicitor;
  - petitions – these are used in respect of winding-up companies, divorce, etc.

Service of the writ
A writ has to be served within four months from the date of issue, but the county court can renew a writ which extends this period.

Rules of service (RSC Ord 6 r 8(1))
Once a writ has been served the defendant must confirm the service, his first action is to acknowledge receipt of the writ within 14 days indicating he wishes to defend the claim.

Judgment in default (Ord 13)
If the defendant does not reply or does not pay in full, the plaintiff can ask for judgment in default. The defendant can have this set aside. (RSC Ord 9 and 13).

Summary judgment (RSC Ord 9 and 13)
The plaintiff can use a summary judgment to declare that the defendant has no defence to the claim. The application for summary judgment is made by *inter partes* summons with an affidavit attached declaring that the plaintiff does not believe that the defendant has a defence to the claim. The defendant can appeal against summary judgment to a judge in chambers or to the Court of Appeal (RSC Ord 2 and 58).

Payment into court (RSC Ord 22)
If a defendant wishes to admit liability but does not agree with the amount the plaintiff is requesting he can make a payment into court. The plaintiff, if he wishes to accept this must do so within 21 days. If the plaintiff does not accept monies paid in by the defendant it is possible he may have to pay both his and the defendant's costs (from the day of paying in) if he is awarded a lesser sum in damages.

Pleadings (RSC Ord 18)
- Statement of claim: the plaintiff can issue a brief outline of his claim against the defendant.
- Defence and counter-claim: here the defendant must, within 14 days of being served with the plaintiff's claim, serve his defence on the plaintiff.
- Reply and defence to counter-claim: if the plaintiff wishes he can reply to the defendant's defence and counter-claim dealing with the issues the defendant has raised.
- Discovery of documents (RSC Ord 24)
  Discovery of documents in civil cases is automatic within 14 days of close of pleadings.

- Security for costs (RSC Ord 23)
  On some occasions the plaintiff may have to pay money into the court to provide for the cost of the action.

The trial
- The plaintiff's case is heard first, his witnesses can be cross-examined by defence counsel. The plaintiff's counsel makes a submission in law at the end of the plaintiff's evidence. The defence witnesses are then called. Defence counsel also makes a closing submission.
- Costs (RSC Ord 62)
  The general rule is that the party who does not succeed must pay the costs of the other party.

Enforcing payment
- Money judgments
  Money judgments are recoverable as is a normal debt, payable from the date of judgment. They can be enforced by *Fieri facias* ('Fi Fa') which is a writ which allows the debtors goods to be seized and sold to meet the debt (Ord 47 RSC).
- Charging order
  A charging order allows the plaintiff to be paid out of specific property (RSC Ord 50).
- Garnishee proceedings
  Garnishee proceedings assign credits of the debtor to the creditor (RSC Ord 49).
- Writ of delivery
  Specific or general, this provides for delivery of goods with the choice of payment for the value of the goods.
- Sequestration
  Sequestration permits sequestrators to enter the defendant's property and take property which is detained until the order is complied with.

County court

Proceedings must take place either:

- in the district in which the defendant lives; or
- where the defendant carries on his business; or
- in the district where the action began.

Default actions are normally used for debt and damages.

Fixed date actions are normally used in claims which are not for money, eg claims in connection with land.

Starting proceedings

The plaintiff must:

- make a request for summons;
- submit with the request two copies of the particulars of claim;
- secure costs if he is under some disability (CCR Ord 10);
- if the plaintiff is receiving legal aid he must present his legal aid certificate;
- if the action is dealing with a personal injury claim he must present a medical report.

The court then issues a summons to the defendant and the plaintiff receives a plaint note from the course.

Pre-trial review

This is held by a district judge to see if there is any way in which the case can be dealt with expediently. The district judge can enter judgment for the plaintiff if the defendant fails to attend.

Pleadings

This is similar to the High Court procedure.

Trial

This again is similar to proceedings in the High Court, the judge is permitted to disallow opening speeches if he so wishes.

Enforcing payment

The most common method of enforcing payment is through a warrant of execution.

- A bailiff makes a first visit within 15 working days of issue of the warrant of execution.
- If the defendant does not pay the amount owed the bailiff can remove and sell items belonging to the defendant to meet the total debt and costs.
- The defendant may be allowed to make payments by instalments (CCR Ord 22).
- The warrant of execution is the same as 'Fi Fa' in the High Court.
- An attachment of earnings can be made which allows the defendant's employers to deduct instalments from his salary (CCR Ord 27).

The Civil Evidence Act 1995

The Civil Evidence Act 1995 (apart from ss 10 and 16(5) which provide for the admissibility of the Ogden Tables) came into force in 31 January 1997. Changes relating to the procedure for admitting hearsay evidence have also been set down in the Rules of the Supreme Court (Amendment) 1996 and the County Court (Amendment No 3) Rules 1996. The Act, it is said, will help to simplify the adducing of hearsay evidence in civil proceedings.

Civil Justice Reform: The Woolf Report

Public confidence in the civil justice system has been eroded by high costs and long delays in bringing a claim before the courts, the present system, it is argued, is failing to meet the needs of litigants. Lord Woolf's Report highlighted the importance of civil justice in the overall legal system and its continued importance in the 21st century. Lord Woolf's proposals for reforming the civil process were published in July 1996 in the shape of two weighty documents, the proposed implementation date being 1 October 1998. Already the Judicial Studies Board is busy on arrangements for the training of the judiciary (which began in April 1997). The Lord Chancellor's Department has produced the Draft Civil Proceedings Rules and are working on rules for specialised areas of civil justice. The main procedural changes are dealt with in Access to Justice; rules advocating changes to the Rules of the Supreme Court 1965 and County Court Rules 1981 are contained in the Draft Civil Proceedings Rules.

The main thrust of Lord Woolf's proposals is to reduce the delay and cost of litigation and to simplify procedures. The Report recommends that control over the progress of cases should be made more the responsibility of the courts. The court should be responsible for procedures and setting timetables for the advancement of the case. Rules for the High Court should be the same, making starting an action in both courts similar. There is advocated small claims jurisdiction up to £5,000, a fast-track procedure with more simplified procedures, fixed timetables and costs are proposed for uncomplicated claims up to £10,000. A new open approach to disclosure of documents by litigants is proposed, as are proposals to help parties who are not legally represented. Proceedings will all start in a similar way to encourage uniformity. Pleadings will be replaced by statements of cases and defences and the plaintiff will be known as the claimant. New rules of the court will render High Court and county court actions uniform and simplify the present rules. It is argued that a pre-litigation programme of negotiation followed by affordable and speedy trial procedures must be the way forward.

There are criticisms of the Woolf reforms, notably put forward by Professor Michael Zander. In his lecture to the Chancery Bar Association on 28 April 1997, Professor Zander asked for some replies to his criticisms of the Woolf reforms. Lord Woolf took the opportunity to reply to Professor Zander in a lecture delivered at the Royal College of Physicians, 13 May 1997. Twenty-one pages of his lecture were given over to a detailed response to Professor Zanders' Chancery Bar Association lecture, where he asserted that 'to pay serious attention to what Professor Zander has said would be to give him credit he does not deserve' – and – 'his lecture was not a balanced consideration of this serious subject and ill considered'. (Zander lecture published in Civil Justice Quarterly July issue.) Professor Zander has commented that 'I am sceptical whether the advantages of having new rules will outweigh the disadvantages'.

Criticism of the reforms has also filtered down from the higher judiciary who are sceptical about the proposals. Further criticism of the proposals has surrounded the funding of the changes. A substantial investment in the court system would have to be made in order for the new system to operate successfully. Whether this will be forthcoming from the new Labour government remains to be seen.

6 Tribunals, inquiries and arbitration

You should be familiar with the following areas:

- administrative tribunals/domestic tribunals
- types and composition of tribunals
- advantages and disadvantages of tribunals
- control on tribunals (1) by the courts (2) by the Council on Tribunals
- the new rules of procedure relating to tribunals
- courts with special jurisdiction
- inquiries
- arbitration

Reasons for the creation of tribunals, inquiries and arbitration

Over the last century many new types of specialised courts and tribunals have been created to deal with specific areas. This is the consequence of increased state involvement into social and economic fields. Because of the technical and special nature of these types of disputes it is thought that the ordinary courts are ill equipped. Further, the procedure of the ordinary courts is slow; administrative decisions need to be made quickly and acted upon in order to maintain efficiency. Delay can also cause extreme financial difficulties for the claimant; quicker and less formal procedures of special tribunals are preferred to the very formal and often very expensive procedures of the ordinary courts.

In certain cases it has been possible to establish a new court, similar to a Division of the High Court, but separate and specifically created to deal with a certain type of dispute.

The Restrictive Practices Court

The Restrictive Practices Act 1976, was established to prevent restrictive trade agreements on matters such as price fixing and restricting the manufacturing or supply of goods. Agreements will only be valid if it can be shown that this would be in the public interest. In order for these decisions to be made, specialised knowledge, unavailable in the ordinary courts, needs to be used. The restrictive practices court usually has 15 members, five of whom are lawyers, the others not. The five lawyers will be three judges of the High Court and one judge from Scotland and Northern Ireland. The other 10 members are appointed on the advice of the Lord Chancellor, each qualified by their knowledge and experience of industry and commerce. Cases are heard by one judge and two lay members sitting together. Points of law are decided by the judge. An appeal is possible on a point of law, heard by the Court of Appeal.

Administrative tribunals

The workload of the ordinary courts is relieved by a large number of tribunals established by an Act of Parliament to settle disputes in specific specialised areas. Tribunals deal with a wide area, social security, employment, land, rents, transport etc. Legal representation tends to be discouraged as legal aid is generally not available and costs are not awarded. As society has progressed certain areas have developed in which complicated disputes can arise. Often these disputes are about administrative matters between government departments and private individuals, hence the term administrative tribunals.

The Tribunals and Inquiries Act

In 1957 a committee was established to examine administrative tribunals in order to produce a set of general principles to regulate and control tribunals. This resulted in the Tribunals and Inquiries Act 1958 and the Council on Tribunals. Because of the sheer number and variety of tribunals and the difference between their roles and procedures it was difficult to create a set of principles and guidelines. However, the Council on Tribunals was established in 1958 to provide as much general guidance as possible. The main function of the Council is to advise and report on the mechanisms and procedures of tribunals. Tribunals are now governed by the Tribunals and Inquiries Act 1971, a consolidating Act, bringing together the previous legislation but only making minor changes (as amended 1992). Members of the Council are appointed by the Lord Chancellor.

Composition of tribunals

Tribunals normally consist of a panel of lay members, with a chairman who does have some legal knowledge. The lack of legal knowledge is not viewed as detrimental because what is required is a cheap, swift informal method of dealing with the dispute, and it is considered, particularly in technical, specialised areas, more desirable that the case is heard by someone expert in that field rather than a lawyer. Under the Trade Union Reform and Employment Rights Act 1993 the tribunal chairman will be called to sit alone to hear certain types of cases.

Statutory tribunals

Social security/welfare
The Social Security Acts provide that benefits shall be paid to people out of state funds in the event of unemployment, sickness, death, maternity and other circumstances. If the persons application is rejected the claimant can appeal to the social security appeal tribunal. It has three members, a chairman who will be legally trained and two lay members. A further appeal lies to the Social Security Commissioner and further to the Court of Appeal on a question of law.

Tribunals dealing with revenue
These tribunals hear appeals against taxation and VAT assessments. The valuation and community charge tribunal, deals with appeals against the community charge.

Land tribunals
There is a host of tribunals who hear complaints related to matters dealing with land eg against compulsory purchase. The land tribunal is an important tribunal with status similar to the High Court.

Tribunals dealing with transportation
The transport tribunal deals with, for example, appeals over road haulage licences. It usually consists of five members, a legally quali-

fied chairman and four lay members with experience in transport matters and experience in commercial matters.

Employment tribunals

Their main role is to deal with disputes which arise from redundancy, complaints of unfair dismissal, discrimination etc. They sit locally with a legally trained chairman and two other lay members, one from a panel representing employers, the other from a panel representing employees. This work is undertaken with the minimum of formality, quickly and efficiently. An appeal lies to the employment appeal tribunal. Industrial tribunals also have to deal with matters relating to discrimination in employment under the Sex Discrimination Act 1975; racial discrimination in employment under the Race Relations Act 1976; issues arising regarding equal pay under the Equal Pay Act 1970 (as amended by the Sex Discrimination Act 1975) and issues related to health and safety under the Health and Safety at Work Act 1974.

The Industrial Tribunals Act 1996 has consolidated the existing legislation in this area. Primary legislation covers matters such as jurisdiction and membership of industrial tribunals, procedures, recoupment of social security benefits and ACAS conciliation. (Previous provisions were contained in Schedule 9 of the EP(C)A 1978.) Also included in the Act are the parallel primary legislative provisions relating to the employment appeal tribunal (previously to be found mainly in Schedule 11 of the EP(C)A 1978).

Mental health review tribunals

These are generally made up of members of medical experts who decide on matters related to medical issues. The tribunal is governed by the Mental Health Act 1983.

Domestic tribunals

These tribunals relate to matters of private rather than public concern and can be established by legislation. Examples of domestic tribunals are committees established to discipline their members. Barristers, for example, are subject to the control of their Inns of Court and the Senate of the Inns of Court and the Bar. Doctors can be struck off their register for unprofessional conduct by the General Medical Council. Other trades and professions subject their members to similar scrutiny. The power that these tribunals have is considerable. Where the tribunal has been set up by statute (such as the Solicitors Act 1974) an appeal will usually lie. In other cases it is dependent on the willingness of the court to get involved, the courts must apply the principles of natural justice, to ensure that the tribunal has not acted *ultra vires* beyond its powers (*Lee v Showmen's Guild of Great Britain* (1952)).

Two members of the defendant guild applied to a local authority for a 'pitch' on a fair ground. Mr Lee obtained the pitch. However, another member, Mr Thaw, who had had the 'pitch' previously decided he should have it again. The rules of the guild enabled the guild to fine a member who operated under 'unfair competition'. Lee was fined and when he had not paid this fine after a month, the guild decided he was no longer a member. Lee applied to the court for a declaration that the guild committee was *ultra vires* and void. The Court of Appeal held that the court had the power to examine the decisions of the guild committee if they involved questions of law, this included interpretation of their rules. It was found the committee had acted *ultra vires* and their decision to expel Mr Lee was void.

Advantages of tribunals

* Speed
  Tribunals operate more quickly than the ordinary courts.
* Cost
  Tribunals are much cheaper than the ordinary courts, there are no fees and costs are not normally awarded.
* Specification
  Tribunals operate in a specialised field, they can establish in a particular area which a court could never achieve.
* Flexibility
  Tribunals are more flexible than courts; they do not have to be constrained by rules of precedence and they have a wide discretion.
* Informality
  Tribunals are less formal than courts. The emphasis is on the encouragement of the individual to bring his own case and not necessarily rely on legal help. The relevant documents and forms do not require legal expertise and the help of the tribunals bench is available to an individual needing assistance. There are no formal rules of evidence that are required in ordinary courts. Evidence can be admitted which for technical reasons would not be available in a court of law. The tribunal chairman has a lot of power and can deformalise the proceedings to make it easier for the applicant.
* Accessibility
  As far as possible tribunals try to be accessible and impartial. It is simpler and quicker to gain access to a tribunal than an ordinary court.

Disadvantages of tribunals

Though there are many obvious advantages to tribunals it is worth remembering that in practice problems have arisen over the years.

- Informality
  It has been difficult to balance both informality and efficiency. Many tribunals have developed very finalised procedures and have become more 'legalised' as more applicants are legally represented and the subject matter of the hearing has become more complex.
- Legal aid
  The unavailability of legal aid leads to an applicant not always being adequately prepared and his case is not always property presented.
- Hearings in private
  Privacy may be a distinct advantage of tribunals but it can be a disadvantage because issues of public importance are not given the publicity necessary under such circumstances.
- Subject matter
  Because the issues that tribunals deal with are often very complex in nature a vast amount of complicated rules have been developed eg social security legislation.
- Appeals
  The appeals' provisions are inadequate. In most cases there is no appeal from a tribunal's decision to a court of law. The right to appeal and the procedure of the appeal are subject to the provisions of the statute under which the tribunal is operating. There is no uniformity in the appeal procedure. The Tribunals and Inquiries Act 1971 provides for any party to appeal *or* to require a tribunal to state a case on a point of law from certain administrative tribunals to the High Court. These appeals can also be heard by the Divisional Court of the Queen's Bench Division. Various other statutes provide the right to appeal to the Supreme Court on points of law, or they can establish a separate appeal tribunal, eg the employment appeal tribunal which hears appeals on points of law from industrial tribunals. Further appeal would lie to the Court of Appeal and House of Lords.
- Bias
  Tribunals can be criticised for being unjust. Although a tribunal is supposed to be independent, it is usually chaired by a person who has an interest, for example, the clerks to Supplementary Benefit Appeals Tribunals are civil servants.

Control of tribunals

The courts

The ordinary courts can exercise some control over tribunals. In the first instance there is usually a provision for a right to appeal on a point of law to the ordinary courts. Occasionally, no right of appeal exists. The courts can exercise some control over tribunals further by the use of 'prerogative' orders, to ensure that the tribunal applies the rules of natural justice.

Mandamus
The performance of some duty, eg the duty of a tribunal to allow an appeal.

Prohibition
This is used to prevent a tribunal going beyond its jurisdiction or acting wrongfully.

Certiorari
This is used to compel a tribunal to inform the High Court of the facts of the case under discussion in order for the High Court to certify whether the tribunal had acted wrongfully, in which case the decision would be quashed. There is no need to ask the High Court for a specific order, a request is made for a judicial review of the decision and the High Court can make such order as it sees fit.

These controls are exercised when the tribunal has acted *ultra vires*; beyond its powers. The courts can insist that the tribunal observe the principles of 'natural justice'; two special rules must be observed.

Audi alterem partem ('hear the other side')
Here there is a duty to hear both sides before a decision is made. This was illustrated in *Ridge v Baldwin* (1963) when a police chief constable who had been suspended from duty pending his trial on corruption charges applied for that suspension to be lifted after his acquittal. The Committee never heard him but turned down his request. The House of Lords held that Mr Ridge ought to have been given 'a fair opportunity of being heard in his own defence'.

Nemo judex in causa sua ('no one should be a judge in his own case')
The decision should be reached after impartial and independent consideration of the evidence. In *Dimes v Grand Junction Canal* (1852) the

judge who heard the case owned shares in the canal company. No allegation of bias was made, the House of Lords stated that the judge, as a shareholder, was disqualified from hearing the case. In *R v Altrincham Justices ex p Pennington* (1975) two men were prosecuted in the magistrates' court for selling vegetables, under the weight specified in the contract, to schools. The chairman of the bench was an alderman who had been co-opted on to the education committee of the local council. The defendants were convicted and made an application for *certiorari* to quash the convictions on the grounds that the magistrate had an interest in the subject matter. The Divisional Court quashed the conviction. In *R v Sussex Justices v P Mc Carthy* (1924) Lord Hewart CJ stated that:

... justice should not only be done but should manifestly and undoubtedly be seen to be done.

Control by the Council on Tribunals

This is a permanent body of up to 15 members appointed by the Lord Chancellor, to keep under review the constitution and working of administrative tribunals and to examine rules of procedure.

The Ombudsman

An official appointed by Parliament to hear complaints from individuals who have suffered administrative mismanagement. Usually the individual complains to his Member of Parliament and he refers the complaint to the Parliamentary Commissioner, who then conducts an inquiry. Similar officials exist for the health service and local government (the Commissioner for Local Administration) dealing with complaints against local authorities and local police authorities. The Ombudsmen system has been introduced into banking and insurance fields, dealing with disputes which arise between the institution and its customers. Under s 21 of the Courts and Legal Services Act 1990 a Legal Services Ombudsman has been appointed by the Lord Chancellor to investigate complaints about professional bodies in the legal profession, eg licensed conveyancers.

Courts with special jurisdiction

Restrictive Practices Court

This court came into being under the Restrictive Trade Practices Act 1956. It was established to monitor contracts which would restrict prices, or restrict the supply of goods and services.

Coroners' Courts

Coroners are appointed by county councils from barristers, solicitors or medical practitioners of at least five years' standing. This office dates from the 12th century. The appointments and jurisdiction of coroners are governed by the Coroners Act 1988. It is a local court, the main function of which is to inquire into deaths if there is reasonable cause to suspect:

- that the dead person suffered a violent or unnatural death; or
- it was a sudden death and the cause was not known; or
- the death occurred in prison.

A jury of seven, nine or 11 can be appointed, the procedure is inquisitorial and witnesses can be compelled to attend.

Courts-martial

Courts-martial deal only with the armed forces. Serious offences are dealt with by courts martials. Very serious cases are dealt with by the ordinary civil courts. The procedure in this court is similar to an ordinary civilian court. The defendant can be represented; there is no jury; the decision is taken by three to five superior officers. There is a court-martial Appeal Court. This is similar to the Court of Appeal.

Ecclesiastical Courts

A historical hierarchy of courts within the church who no longer have any jurisdiction over laymen.

Future and control of the tribunal system

The Council on Tribunals is over 30 years old and has endeavoured to promote some coherence into the tribunal system, emphasising the aims of openness, fairness and impartiality advocated by the Franks Committee in 1957. The use of tribunals has grown over the years and the different types of tribunals covering varied areas of specialism is expanding, additions such as the banking appeal tribunal; the financial services tribunal; the copyright tribunal and valuation and community charge tribunals are examples.

It is argued, however, that control and supervision of the system cannot rest with one body alone. Though the courts do exercise some control through appeal or review, it is argued that there needs to be a uniform code of procedure to govern the workings of tribunals to promote more safeguards and consistency. The questions asked are should the Council of Tribunals be given extended powers? Should its composition be altered and its resources increased? Should it be afforded a political base in the form of a Select Committee in Parliament? Various reports have drawn attention to issues concerning the tribunal system. These include, as well as the Franks Report and Annual Reports of the Council of Tribunals, the Special Report of the Council in 1980, 'The Functions of the Council on Tribunals (Cmnd 7805); and The Justice/All Souls Report, 'Administrative Justice' in 1988.

The 1980 Report recommended, *inter alia*:

- a statutory restatement of the requirements of consultation on procedural rules;
- an obligation on Ministers to disclose the substance of advice offered by the council on primary of secondary legislation;
- a wider and uniform entitlement to offer advice on tribunals or inquiries; and
- a specific power to attend private hearings of tribunals under the Council's supervision and to attend the deliberation stage of proceedings of such tribunals.

These proposals did not find favour with the Lord Chancellor.

The 1988 Report called for an Administrative Review Commission, a body which would keep under constant review all the procedures and institutions whereby the individual could challenge administrative action. Several commentators have argued in favour of this stating that:

... the strands of administrative law should be pulled together and considered in an national and international perspective. This could bring in co-operation with similar advisory bodies in other countries and the capacity to take account of developments in Europe, not least with regard to the European Convention on Human Rights, and in the wider field of international law.

(DGT Williams (1988) *Civil Justice Quarterly* p 32)

There is no doubt that the tribunal system is a valued resource. But it is in need of change if it is to be part of a unified system of justice. The links with government departments need to be severed, more systematic training is necessary and a duty needs to be placed on the tribunal to give reasons for its decision to enable the parties involved, and the Court of Appeal, to see if the law has been applied properly; new rules of procedure have been implemented in respect of confidentiality and to try to save time by reducing the number of cases going to full time tribunal hearings.

Industrial Tribunal (Constitution and Rules of Procedure) Regulations 1993

The new Industrial Tribunal Rules of Procedure replace the 1985 Rules of Procedure. These new rules make substantive changes including tribunals taking a more inquisitorial approach when making decisions and provisions to ensure that privacy is maintained in cases dealing with sexual matters.

Provisions regarding the originating application remain the same. In cases dealing with sexual issues r 2(2) permits the secretary to the tribunals to leave out of tribunal documents any information which might lead the public to identify parties in the proceedings.

Rule 4(3) empowers the tribunal to ask any party to provide a written answer to questions if it believes this will benefit the proceedings by making issues clearer; either party in the proceedings can require this. This widens the scope that the tribunals already have to require a party to explain more clearly the originating application; this goes further in asking a party to answer more fully questions which are relevant to the proceedings. Rule 7(4) permits the tribunal to conduct a pre-hearing review in which the tribunal can require a party to pay a deposit in order to continue with the hearing, if the tribunal thinks that the party has no real chance of succeeding with the case. The paying of the deposit will allow the party to proceed or contest the proceedings. The party must forward the deposit within 21 days or the tribunal can dismiss the proceedings. Requests for an extension of the 21 days period can be granted by the tribunal (for a further 14 days). Before the tribunal can request the party to pay a deposit they must have examined the circumstances of the party and whether the party can afford to pay a deposit. Each party to the proceedings must be informed that the party paying the deposit could be liable for an award of costs made against him and that he may lose his deposit if he insists on continuing with the proceedings. He will be entitled to have his deposit returned if the tribunal finds against him on an issue which was not considered at the pre-trial review. Tribunals can hold pre-trial reviews in all cases. To reduce the risk of prejudice members of a tribunal who attend the pre-trial review cannot then sit at the full hearing. The rules relating to the actual hearing have changed little, but there are changes to the procedure at a hearing emphasising a more investigatory role for the tribunal. Rule 9(1) allows the tribunal to 'make such enquiries of persons appearing before it and witnesses as it considers appropriate'. Rule 10(3) requires the tribunal to give an explanation of how an award made was calculated, the tribunal is also required to give reasons for the decision in full, particularly in cases of sex and racial discrimination and equal pay, or when the tribunal is specifically asked to do so. Changes have also been made to payment of costs. Wide scope has been given to the tribunal to make a cost order in cases where a party has behaved badly. Under r 14(1) the tribunal can make a restricted reporting order in cases where allegations of sexual offences are made. This is to protect the parties in the proceedings by making sure that while the case is being heard the press cannot identify parties to the proceedings fostering greater confidentiality.

As industrial tribunals celebrated the 25th anniversary of the right not to be unfairly dismissed, the continued debate regarding their future raged on. The main issue concerning tribunals is not their lack of success, on the contrary, it is because of that success that problems have arisen. The number of claims dealt with by tribunals have more than doubled in the five years from 1989–94, resulting in a huge drain on public funds. Tribunals, it is argued, have moved away from the aims that they were set up to serve. Far from a quick, cheap, and simple form of justice, the tribunal system has become overburdened, complicated, too legalistic and shares many of the problems associated with the court system they were set up to circumvent. Faced with mounting criticism of the tribunal system the government instituted a review of the system to consider the alternatives to help relieve the growing pressures on tribunals and reduce the financial public fund burden. This review cumulated in a consultative document 'Resolving Employment Rights Disputes: Draft Legislation for Consultation', which was published by the Department of Trade and Industry in July 1996. The view that the government took was that litigation through the tribunal system should be a last resort and more should be made of the alternative systems of arbitration and mediation with greater powers going to ACAS to help resolve employment disputes.

The consultation document became a draft bill in the autumn but was not included in the Queen's Speech owing to pressure with the run up to the general election. The Labour government has agreed that reform of tribunals is necessary. It is still, however, uncertain what shape this reform will take.

Inquiries

Inquiries are usually set up on an *ad hoc* basis when it is necessary to deal with a specific issue eg inquiries to investigate major accidents by air, sea or rail; inquiries to investigate companies under the Companies Act and inquiries into a specific event. The Minister concerned will usually set up the inquiry and powers will be conferred to summon witnesses, compel documents etc. Inquiries usually serve to find the cause of a problem through the establishment of factual information. Supervision of inquiries is by the Council on Tribunals. Inquiries are governed by the rules of natural justice.

Arbitration

Arbitration is a means of settling disputes other than by court action and arises when one or more persons are appointed to hear the arguments put forward by the parties and to decide upon them. A judge in an ordinary court of law does in fact arbitrate (meaning to decide). However, the difference between arbitration and a court of law is that the arbitrator can add a deeper understanding of the practical issues in a particular field as well as bringing some legal knowledge to bear on the procedures.

Advantages of arbitration

Arbitration can be conducted in private, therefore no publicity is attached to the proceedings. Arbitration could possibly be cheaper for the parties. Arbitration can lead to quicker solutions to the dispute. A matter can be referred to arbitration:

By the court
The court can refer a matter before it to arbitration, eg if it concerns very technical issues or specialised difficulties.

By Act of Parliament

Certain statutes provide for arbitration, eg disputes between employee/employer.

By agreement

The parties themselves may agree to submit to arbitration either at the start of their contract in anticipation of a possible dispute, or after a dispute has arisen.

Agreements

Agreements can be in writing or oral, however, the Arbitration Act, only applies to those in writing. Agreements normally specify the arbitrator. However, the agreement can specify that a third party name the arbitrator, eg a trade or professional body. The arbitrator can examine the parties and witnesses on oath, and call on parties to produce documents, accounts, etc.

The award

The award of the arbitrator is final, there is no appeal. The arbitrator can award costs. Where there is an arbitration agreement in operation and one party nevertheless institutes court proceedings the court can stay the proceedings on an application from the other party. The arbitration must cover the dispute which is before the court and the party seeking the stay must have taken no part in the court proceedings.

Procedure in arbitration

It is the duty of the arbitrator to settle the dispute by making an award. The arbitrator, if he so wishes, can employ a legal advisor to help him make the award if he feels he lacks competence or expertise to deal with the legal issues involved.

The arbitrator is responsible for setting the time and place for hearing the parties and informs the parties of this. If one party does not attend the arbitrator can proceed in his absence.

Unlike a judge, if the arbitrator has sufficient expertise and knowledge of the practice of the trade in which the dispute has occurred he can waive the need for expert witnesses. This helps to reduce the costs of the proceedings.

If an important point of law arises, the arbitrator has the power to 'state a cause' for the deliberation of the court. He will relate the facts of the case and determine the questions on which the court has to decide when the opinion of the court is obtained. The arbitrator applies the law to the facts of the case and gives his award.

If the arbitrator declines to 'state a case' for the opinion of the court, a party to the arbitration proceedings can compel him to do so.

The award is final and no appeal is possible. However, the court can set aside an award by the arbitrator on procedural grounds, for example:

- if the arbitrator refused to hear one of the parties (*audi alterem partem*);
- witnesses are examined in the absence of one of the parties, thus affording no opportunity to cross-examine;
- if the arbitrator has been in communication with one of the parties regarding the subject matter referred to arbitration;
- if the arbitrator has accepted a bribe or has a personal interest he fails to disclose.

Enforcement

The party in whose favour an arbitration award is made can enforce the award in the same way as he can enforce a court judgment, but only if the court consents.

Alternative dispute resolution

The Practice Note (1996) (QBD Commercial Courts) advocates the use of alternative dispute resolution in the Commercial Court to save litigant's time and reduce costs, to reduce delay and promote greater choice of remedies.

7 The jury

You should be familiar with the following areas:
- criticisms of the jury system
- the role of the jury
- selection of the jury
- challenging jury membership
- jury vetting
- the Royal Commission's proposals relating to the jury

The jury system

It has long been thought that the jury is one of the most vital features of the English legal system and a fundamental safeguard to our liberty. However, confidence in the institution is waning and has been the subject of criticism in recent studies:

- 'The Jury Under Attack' (1988) Findly and Duff
- 'Taking Liberties: The Criminal Jury in the 1990s' (1991) Enright and Morton
- 'The Lamp that shows that Freedom Lives – is it Worth a Candle?', Penny Darbyshire (1991) *Criminal Law Review* p 740
- 'Notes of a Lawyer Juror', Penny Darbyshire (1990) *New Law Journal* p 2164.

The most influential of the recent articles is Penny Darbyshire's 'The Lamp that shows that Freedom Lives – is it Worth a Candle?', which was produced as a result of her experience of serving on a jury. Her aim was:

... to question the traditional qualifications used in praise and defence of the jury, suggesting that some of them are conceptually unsound. I argue that jury defenders inflate the jury's importance by portraying the 'right' to jury trial as central to the criminal justice system and as a guardian of due process and civil liberties.

She further argues that:

The jury has probably provoked more comment and research than any other component of the criminal justice system. It seems to attract the most praise and the least theoretical analysis.

Darbyshire criticises the traditional view of the jury and criticises those commentators who emphasise the mystery of the jury. Juries, she states, are not a representative sample of the population, she points out that they are 'an antidemocratic, irrational and haphazard legislator, whose erratic and secret decisions run counter to the rule of law'.

The Runciman Commission have put forward proposals to reduce the role of the jury in criminal trials but these proposals have met with indignant comments.

However, it is true that although the jury has been seen as an important cornerstone of the English legal system there have been few in-depth studies of it. Commentators have tended to view the jury in a romantic light, which, it is argued is detrimental to change in the justice process. Darbyshire's arguments tend to imply that the jury system plays such a small role in the minority of cases anyway, its passing would not really be seen as any great loss. Others argue however, that the jury system performs a service which would be difficult to replace and the jury should be protected at all costs.

The use of the jury in English law goes back far into history. However, it was not until the beginning of the 19th century that it was determined that jurors should not have personal knowledge of the accused; until the 18th century the juror's function was more or less to help the judge with an assessment of the defendant's character. The use of jurors, has, however, declined in recent years. The Administration of Justice Act 1933 limited the use of juries in civil cases, juries are more prominent in defamation and fraud cases. In 1986 the Roskill Report advocated the abolition of a right to jury trial in complex fraud cases. They asserted that fraud cases are long with a great deal of complex evidence. The Committee stated that:

The background against which the frauds are alleged to have been committed, the sophisticated world of high finance and international trading, is probably a mystery to more or less all of the jurors, its customs and practices a closed book. Even the language in which the allegedly fraudulent transactions have been conducted will be unfamiliar. A knowledge of accountancy or book-keeping may be essential to an understanding of the case. If any juror has such knowledge it is by chance.

(Report of the Fraud Trials Committee, 1986, para 8.21)

Lord Denning has argued that some jurors are not adequately suited to the task required of them. In 'Safeguarding Trial by Jury' (1988) *The Times* he commented on the incident when some jurors were intimidated during a trial in Leeds Crown Court:

You may get girls or lads of 18 serving on a jury who may be an easy prey to bribery or intimidation.

The role of the jury

The jury's function during a trial is to decide the facts of the case. They are laypersons and have no knowledge of law and are not competent to put forward any opinion on law. They have to rely upon their common sense to assess the accused and the evidence against him in order to reach a verdict. It is the judge's function, *inter alia*, to explain the law to the jury and they reach a verdict through their understanding of the law explained by him. The relationship between a judge and a jury is very influential. The judge conducts the trial and controls the evidence the jury is allowed to hear. If the evidence is weak the judge can instruct the jury to acquit the accused. At the conclusion of the evidence the judge will sum up the case to the jury before they retire to reach a verdict. The judge at this point can do no more. The judge can use his summing up to indicate to the jury that the only reasonable decision to reach would be a guilty verdict, however, there is no actual judicial power to instruct juries to convict an accused (*DPP v Stonehouse* (1978)). If the jury's verdict is a perverse one there is nothing more the judge can do; it must be accepted. If the verdict is an acquittal, it is unchallengeable. There is no appeal against an acquittal at the Crown Court and further, once the accused is acquitted, he cannot be charged with the same offence again.

This has been criticised and was particularly highlighted during the case where the accused was found not guilt of murder on the grounds of self defence (*R v Elliot* (1993)). The case attracted much media attention and helped to fuel the debate for those commentators wishing to see a limitation on the powers of the jury.

However, Baldwin and McConville in *Jury Trial* (1979) found no evidence to suggest that juries acquitted people in the face of unjust prosecution. They argued that perverse verdicts occurred at random, and that the jury had the disadvantage of being unpredictable. The notion of the jury applying its own equity thus appears to have no substance.

Section 36 of the Criminal Justice Act 1972 does provide for a procedure whereby points of law which arise in a criminal case where the defendant has been acquitted can be referred to the Court of Appeal by the Attorney General to see if any loopholes in the law can be amended. This does not, however, affect the actual verdict of the case. An appeal does lie in civil law to overturn a jury's verdict, but only in circumstances where the jury has come to such an unreasonable decision that no reasonable verdict could have reached.

Selection of the jury

The Criminal Justice Act 1972 abolished the property qualifications for jurors. Today anyone who is listed on the electoral register between the ages of 18 and 70 is eligible for jury service. The Juries Act 1974 lays down the rules for selecting a jury.

Persons eligible for jury service

Those eligible for jury service must be aged between 18 and 70, on the electoral roll, who have been resident in the UK for at least five years since the age of 13. (The Criminal Justice Act 1987 allows as of right excusal to those aged over 65.)

Persons ineligible

Ineligible persons are members of the judiciary and others involved in the justice system eg barristers and solicitors; the clergy, the mentally ill. Section 40 of the Criminal Justice and Public Order Act 1994 disqualifies from service any person who is on bail in criminal proceedings.

Those disqualified

Persons who are disqualified are those who have been sentenced to more than five years in prison and anyone who has served a prison sentence of three months or more in the last 10 years. Section 40 of the Criminal Justice and Public Order Act 1994 disqualifies from service any person who is on bail in criminal proceedings.

Those entitled to be excused
Members of Parliament
Members of Armed Forces
Members of Medical or Legal Professions

Those entitled to be excused by administrative discretion
Those entitled to be excused by administrative discretion are those
persons who have served on a jury in the last two years and persons
with good reasons to be excused (s 120 of the Criminal Justice Act
1988).

Challenging jury membership

The defence can challenge the presence of a juror on three grounds:
Under s 12(4) of the Juries Act 1974:

- the juror is in fact not qualified; or
- the juror is biased; or
- the juror may be reasonably suspected of bias against the defendant.

The prosecution have a right to challenge as well as the defence. The
prosecution have a right to ask a juror to 'stand by' for the Crown. The
Attorney General has laid down guidelines as to when the prosecution
should exercise this right:

- if a jury check shows information to support exercising the right to
  stand by; or
- if the person to be sworn in as a juror is unsuitable and the defence
  agree.

Either side can 'challenge the array', or suggest that the whole jury
panel has been improperly assembled.

Peremptory challenge

The defence used to have a right of peremptory challenge whereby
they could challenge up to three jurors without giving any reasons at
all. The maximum number of peremptory challenges used to be seven;
this was reduced to three under the Criminal Law Act 1977 because of
abuse of the procedure. The right to peremptory challenge has now
been abolished by s 118 of the Criminal Justice Act 1988.

Jury vetting

The panel is selected at random and any party to the proceedings can inspect the panel from which the jurors will be chosen. Jury vetting is the investigation of jurors' backgrounds to determine whether they are suitable for jury service. Jury vetting is a very controversial issue. The practice first came to the public notice in 1978 during the 'ABC Trial' a case brought under the Official Secrets Act 1911. It was revealed that the process of jury vetting was allowed by guidelines drawn up by the Attorney General. These guidelines, advocated that jury vetting was to be allowed only in exceptional cases such as terrorism, cases involving the Official Secrets Acts and 'professional' criminals. The consent of the DPP was necessary and the Attorney General had to be informed. Two cases in 1980 highlighted the practice of jury vetting.

In R v Crown Court at Sheffield ex p Brownlow (1980) Judge Pickles allowed two policemen charged with assault the right to vet the jury panel. He ordered the Chief Constable of South Yorkshire to supply to the defendant's solicitors details of any previous convictions of members of the jury panel. The Chief Constable applied for *certiorari*, but was unsuccessful. Lord Denning in the Court of Appeal felt that the order of the judge had been a bad one and that on balance the Court of Appeal had the power to quash the judge's order, the Divisional Court having declined to do so. However, Shaw and Brandon LJJ thought otherwise. Lord Denning stated that:

To my mind it is unconstitutional to engage in 'jury vetting' ... If this sort of thing is to be allowed what comes of a man's right of privacy?

In *R v Mason* (1980) the Court of Appeal upheld as lawful the practice of Northamptonshire Police of checking to see if any members of a jury panel had a criminal record and cast doubt on the view expressed in *Brownlow*.

It is argued that the constitutional position of this practice is much in doubt and has been greatly criticised. However, the legitimacy and that of the Crown's right to 'stand by' potential jurors is clearly stated by the Court of Appeal in *R v Bettaney* (1985).

The Attorney General, following a Practice Note in 1988, issued a statement confirming the previous guidelines subject to three main provisions:

- checks on Special Branch records would only be allowed on the authority of the Attorney Generals following a recommendation of the DPP;

- there would be no 'vetting' in cases of strong political motives unless they concerned terrorism; and
- cases involving security would only be checked where there was threat to national security.

However, whether these guidelines are adhered to or are merely paid lip service is debatable. In 1985, a civil servant, Clive Ponting, was acquitted under s 2 of the Official Secrets Act 1911. In this case 60 potential jurors were vetted by MI5. There appeared to be no threat to national security involved.

Arguments for retaining the jury

- The jury is selected at random and is thus in a better position to reflect the views of society.
- To establish facts is a matter of common sense and requires no legal training, having a broader range of opinions also helps to overcome individual bias.
- The jury is less 'prosecution minded' than judges or magistrates.
- The jury is considered to be the 'bulwark of individual liberties' and the public have confidence in the present system of criminal trials.
- Juries indicate the extent of public feeling on the state of the law.
- The jury can check abuses of judicial power.

Arguments against retaining the jury

- Juries are uneducated in the law and find it difficult to weigh evidence properly, particularly in complex fraud cases.
- The law of evidence can be distorted in order to prevent the jury forming prejudices against the accused (eg the accused's past criminal record even though it is not relevant to the case).
- A good lawyer can too easily sway a jury.
- It is not totally possible to prevent jurors from being bribed etc.
- Juries often bring in perverse verdicts.
- Juries acquit too many people out of prejudice, ignorance and bullying in the retiring room.

The Runciman Commission

The Royal Commission on Criminal Justice made recommendations in order to try and improve the jury system. One important factor which was recommended was that s 8 of the Contempt of Court Act 1981 should be repealed. This would allow research into the jury and then reasons for their verdicts. It is traditional that the decision-making process of the jurors remains secret. This is to ensure protection for the jury, to prevent any outside influences and prejudices affecting the fairness of the verdict. It is argued that if juries were required to give reasons for the decisions they reached it would place undue pressure on the jurors and would inevitably affect the verdict. However, if the jury is considered to be the cornerstone of justice, as many commentators argue, then surely more research into juries is necessary, the repealing of s 8 would allow this. The Commission also made recommendations regarding the selection and disqualification of jurors. They stated that the electoral registers should contain all members of the public who qualify to be listed. This would, however, be a mammoth task as many people actively chose not to be registered on the electoral roll. Further, they suggested that if a juror is unable to attend on a particular day they should then be given an alternative date. Remuneration for jury duties needs to be looked at, it can be expensive if an individual has to attend court and expenses granted to jurors at present are not adequate. The Commission also recommended more checks to ensure that jurors did not know one another or the accused. Jurors should be required to admit to any previous convictions they may have and be prosecuted for any false declarations made. More screening of jurors was necessary. The Commission recommended that at least three members of the jury should be from ethnic minority communities and that the defence or prosecution should be able to insist that one of these members is from the same ethnic minority group as the accused. With regard to the proceedings the Commission recommended that jurors need to be protected from any outside intimidation. If a trial is expected to last a long time judges should be able to schedule the trial to enable the juror to attend at his workplace.

One of the most controversial recommendations put forward by the Commission was the abolition of the defendant's right to elect for jury trial in 'either way' cases. The right to elect jury trial by the defendant in an 'either way' case should be taken from the accused and placed in the jurisdiction of the magistrates. This would promote 'a more rational distribution of cases'. It is argued that this proposal is rational if viewed from an economic standpoint since it is cheaper to conduct a trial in a magistrates' court than in the Crown Court. However, some commentators, such as McConville criticise this view. They argue that if a defendant is charged with a serious offence which could have serious implications for him then he should have the right to a jury trial. McConville argues that:

It is one thing for a defendant to decide, usually on the basis of independent advice, to waive that right ... it is another for the State to abolish that right altogether, and to assign the decision to magistrates, who under current court financing arrangements may have other pressures on them to retain cases.

('A Comedy of Errors' (1993) *Legal Action*)

The Commission recommended that:

In cases involving 'either way' offences the defendant should no longer have the right to insist on a trial by jury. Where the CPS and the defendant agree that the case is suitable for summary trial, it should proceed to trial in a magistrates' court, the case should go to the Crown Court for trial if both the prosecution and defence agree that it should be tried on indictment. Where the defence do not agree with the CPS's proposal on which court should try the case, the matter should be referred to the magistrates for a decision.

McConville asserts that:

64% of either way cases sent to the Crown Court are sent by magistrates presumably on the basis that they regard the case as too serious or their sentencing powers insufficient. Yet in 62% of these cases the magistrates could have imposed the sentence imposed by the Crown Court. This shows their irrationality.

However, Michael Zander assets that the Commission's recommendation deals not with the 64% of either way offences which are sent to the Crown Court but with the other 36% where the defendant opts for Crown Court trial.

McConville argues that:

Michael Zander says the Commission's proposal was intended to deal only with defendants who elect Crown Court trial and then plead guilty (around 6% of those who face election). If so then the Commission has been incompetent as well as misguided, since the effect will be to deny many of those who contest either way cases through to jury trial, a fair proportion of whom are acquitted the right to do so.

Further he asserts that:

A Commission less concerned with administrative convenience might have considered how more defendants who presently plead guilty at Crown Court could be encouraged to take their cases to full jury trial, rather than cutting them out of this right altogether.

('A Comedy of Errors' (1993) *Legal Action*)

There is empirical evidence to suggest that defendants prefer to be tried by a jury due to the belief that magistrates are on the side of the police and are harder on defendants than a jury is. Magistrates are all too ready to believe prosecution evidence and thus are not trusted to try cases fairly.

The Commission's report stated that the accused should not 'be able to choose their court of trial solely on the basis that they think that they will get a fairer hearing at one level than another'.

Michael Zander argues that:

The commission was well aware of the belief that magistrates are not as favourable to defendants as juries. It also accepted that the 'quality of justice' is probably lower in magistrates' courts. Even the most passionate defender of our system of magistrates' courts would accept that. It is, after all implicit in having one tier for the masses of cases and a higher tier for the more serious cases.

('An Error of Judgment' (1993) *Legal Action*)

The Royal Commission in their proposals relating to the jury appear to reinforce the view that the jury is seen in an artificial romanticised light and that it is necessary to reduce its role in the criminal justice system. In recent years the jury system has become an object of distrust; many cases have already been taken out of the control of the jury system. Reforms to the Criminal Damage Act 1971 have made these cases, to all intent and purpose, summary offences. (Hedderman & Moxon 'Magistrates' Court or Crown Court' Mode of Trial Decisions and Sentencing (1992).) Further, Part V of the Criminal Justice Act 1988 removed the right to jury trial in either way offences, including driving whilst disqualified. In their study 'The Distribution of Criminal Business between the Crown Court and Magistrates' Courts' (1975) the James Committee recommended that minor thefts and similar offences should become summary offences. The jury in civil cases has almost gone and the jury in the Coroner's Court has been modified by the Criminal Law Act 1977. The Northern Ireland (Emergency Provisions) Act 1991 has taken away the right to jury trial for defendants in serious criminal cases and it is possible for a judge to curtail the jury by asking for a special verdict (*R v Bourne* (1953); *R v Robbins* (1988)). Therefore, it can be seen that the power of the jury system has been curtailed over the years, the Royal Commission's proposals will certainly add to this.

Some commentators advocate that reform of English Criminal procedures should be in line with continental procedures. Indeed, the Royal Commission conducted a study of pre-trial procedures used in France and Germany (Leigh and Zedner, 'A Report on the Administration of Criminal Justice in the Pre-trial Phase in France and Germany' (1992)). This view has gained favour in recent years, but it is doubtful whether the idea of reforming the English jury based on the continental system would be a viable alternative.

Reform

The use of civil juries has declined sharply since the 19th century (under 400 trials per year) and commentators arguing for the reduction of the use of juries in the criminal process are gaining strength. A recent Home Office report 'Review of Delay in the Criminal Justice System' (1997) has called for changes in the use of juries in the criminal justice process. The report claims, *inter alia*, that the defendant should no longer be able to call into question the decision of a magistrate to hear a case. Further, indictable offences should be heard in the Crown Court rather than going through the procedures of the magistrates' court. By restricting the use of juries the high costs of providing this 'trial by one's peers' would be saved and the process speeded up considerably. However, many civil libertarians hotly dispute the evidence put forward in the report and the debate whether juries should be retained goes on.

8 Legal services

You should be familiar with the following areas:

- legal aid and advice
- rising costs in the legal aid system
- eligibility for legal aid
- Legal Aid Act 1988
- Legal Aid Board
- civil and criminal legal aid
- legal aid franchising
- legal aid for children
- criticisms of the legal aid scheme
- unmet legal need
- alternative legal services

Legal aid and advice

The cost of litigation through the courts can be a very expensive experience. However, if it is the only way of solving a dispute the parties may have no alternative. The concept of access to justice for all is seen as being central to our notion of the Rule of Law and it is therefore vital that nobody should be denied the right to have their case heard before a court because they cannot afford the cost of litigation. Although lawyers have been the butt of many jibes that they are interested only in charging high fees and getting rich quickly, it was indeed the lawyers themselves who first advanced the concept of 'legal aid' as we know it today. Before any financial assistance scheme was set up lawyers would sometimes take on a case for no fee at all, or for a bare fee, hardly meeting their expenses. There was also the traditional 'dock brief' where an accused in a criminal case could select a barrister who was in court, but not representing a client, and the barrister was duty bound to represent the defendant. It was not until 1903 under the Poor Prisoners' Defence Act that lawyers were paid out of public funds. In 1949 the Legal Aid and Advice Act allowed for state funded representation in civil courts. This was introduced on the recommendations of the Rushcliffe Committee who advanced the idea that legal aid should be available not just for the poor but also for those individuals of moderate means. With regard to criminal cases the Committee decided legal aid should be available if necessary in keeping with the interests of justice. This came about because of a change in society's attitudes after the Second World War, the proposals being along similar lines as the National Health Service. However, unlike the National Health Service, legal aid was to be means tested. Lord Denning commented on the legal aid system:

I have often said that since the Second World War the greatest revolution in the law has been the system of legal aid. It means that in many cases the lawyers' fees and expenses are paid for by the State and not by the party concerned.

The State system of legal aid was created through a series of statutes:

- Legal Aid and Advice Act 1949
- Legal Aid Act 1964
- Criminal Justice Act 1967
- Legal Advice and Assistance Act 1972
- Legal Aid Act 1974
- Legal Aid Act 1979 (as amended by the Administration of Justice Act 1985)
- Legal Aid Act 1988

Rising legal aid costs

During the 1980s the cost of the legal aid scheme was escalating in 1986 legal aid cost nearly £400 million; in 1991 £698 million; and in 1993 it rose to £857 million. It was argued that drastic cuts had to be made in the legal aid scheme and in 1986 the Legal Aid Scrutiny Commission published a report in which it recommended a number of proposals to save costs on the administration of the scheme. Some of these proposals were implemented in the Legal Aid Act 1988. More recently, the Lord Chancellor in the Legal Aid Consultation paper 1991, set out five proposals to alter the funding of legal aid:

- litigants funding by self-sacrifice;
- reduced interest bank loans;
- contingency fees;
- legal insurance; and
- the safety net (whereby the cost of the litigation is on the plaintiff until a set figure is reached and only then will legal aid be made available).

Over the last few years legal aid has been the subject of much debate as a desperately needed solution to the problem is sought. There appears to be no clear policy, accept, perhaps, the fact that there is no actual right to be legally assisted. The Lord Chancellor has faced much criticism over his legal aid eligibility cuts but has not flinched and seems determined to press ahead with them despite severe criticisms from the Lord Chief Justice and the Legal Aid Advisory Committee. A report from the Legal Aid Board in 1991 asserted that since 1981 the legal aid scheme has been developing rapidly at the rate of 17% a year. Three-fifths of this increase was due to the increase in the amount of cases and two-fifths due to the rise in the administration of the scheme.

Reasons for increases

It is not difficult to explain why there is an increase in the number of cases. The number of crimes recorded has risen from around 1 per 100 population in the 1950s to 5 per 100 population in the 1970s and to 7.4 per 100 population in 1989 (Home Office Research Statistics 1991). This means that with the increased crime rate and police involvement in the criminal courts, these are inevitable increases in criminal legal aid. The soaring divorce rate led to many more cases in civil proceedings which often involved complicated and protracted litigation over property rights. The burgeoning legal aid system needed tighter controls placed upon it in order to make it more efficient and cost-effective. Lord Mackay warned of the deep incisions which would have to be made in the legal aid scheme. The intended cuts (the first in the 44 years of life of the legal aid scheme) it is estimated, will affect between 12 and 14 million people, affecting 37% of households.

Eligibility for legal aid

Whether an individual is eligible for legal aid will depend upon the individual's financial circumstances. In keeping with the 1949 Act the poor have always been able to obtain legal aid. It is the person of 'moderate means' who finds himself in a position of uncertainty as to whether he would qualify under the scheme. At the beginning of the legal aid scheme the majority of the population were eligible for legal aid because of their low incomes. However, as wage levels increased and more women started to enter employment and earn an income, its percentage of eligibility declined. The legal aid limits were set at the same level as supplementary benefits in 1974 and increased each year as a result. However, it was argued that because of the spiralling costs in civil litigation and higher income limits imposed in personal injury cases in 1990, 11 million adults lost their eligibility entitlement to legal assistance between 1979 and 1990 (Michael Murphy, 'Civil Legal Aid Eligibility Estimates' (1990)).

Legal aid eligibility criteria

There have been changes to the eligibility criteria for legal advice and assistance introduced in April 1997.

Under the Green Form scheme the disposable *income* limit has been raised from £72 to £77 per week. The *capital* limit of £1,000 (no dependants) remains the same. ABWOR disposable income limit is raised from £162 to £166 per week, with contributions starting if weekly disposable income exceeds £69.

Civil legal aid

To qualify for civil legal aid an applicant must have a disposable *income* of less than £2,563 per year (unless in receipt of income support) and a disposable *capital* of less than £3,000 (no dependants). Contributions will be required if the applicant has a disposable *income* of between £2,563 and £7,595 per year. In personal injury cases, the upper *income* limit is £8,370. Contributions will also be required if the applicant has a disposable *capital* of between £3,000 and £6,750 per year. In personal injury cases, the upper *capital* limit is £8,560.

The statutory charge

This was introduced as a method of restricting access to legal aid. The statutory charge allowed the legal aid fund to charge any property which was recovered or preserved by the litigant during proceedings.

Section 16(6) of the Legal Aid Act 1988 states that:

Except so far as regulations otherwise provide (a) any sums remaining unpaid on account of a person's contribution in respect of the sums payable by the Board and in respect of any proceedings; and (b) a sum equal to any deficiency by reason of his total contributions being less than the net liability of the

Board on his account, shall be a first charge for the benefit of the Board on any property which is recovered or preserved for him in the proceedings.

The introduction of the statutory charge was centred around the motion of the private paying client; the idea of individuals bearing no relation, fighting it out, each with equal resources, each having made a rational calculation of the costs involved. But this can hardly be attributed to matrimonial cases which are different from normal civil litigation. Matrimonial disputes involve individuals who have been intimately involved with one another, and are charged with deep emotional feelings. Children may be involved in the dispute, adding to the difficulties since the parties will have to maintain a future contact in order to see the children. This is far removed from the cold, impassive, gladiators envisaged in ordinary civil disputes. This was recognised by the report from the Lord Chancellor's Advisory Committee on Legal Aid (1983/84) which stated that:

Matrimonial disputes are emotional as much as rational ... People fight matrimonial issues for reasons of anger, pride, revenge, etc as much as for motives of financial gain.

The property or financial gain in a matrimonial dispute will almost certainly depreciate as the individual has to meet the costs of legal representation and litigation. Further, there are no winners in matrimonial cases, the courts do not seek to blame either of the parties, but to try and bring an amicable end to a traumatic situation.

The statutory charge therefore manifests injustice in circumstances where the parties have already suffered emotional and physical costs. In Stuart v The Law Society (1987) a wife, receiving legal aid, accepted a lump sum payment of £7,000, relinquishing her right to receive periodical payments of £1,820 a year. However, the woman had not considered that she had put herself in a position were she was liable to pay her own costs through the statutory charge. These costs amounted to a considerable amount leaving the woman with a very small sum. This is but one example of how the statutory charge can ambush litigants and cause hardship in the long term (see further Hanlon v The Law Society (1981)).

The Legal Aid Act 1988

The present legislation is contained in the Legal Aid Act 1988. This enables the Lord Chancellor to make regulations which will meet the public need for legal aid. The Act came into force in 1989 and repealed all earlier legislation in this area. Section 1 of the Act sets out the intentions of the legislation which are to create a 'framework' of legal advice and assistance which will be publicly funded.

Legal Aid Board

The scheme is administered by the Legal Aid Board which was established by s 3 of the Legal Aid Act 1988. The Legal Aid Board is a quango, incorporated to establish a Legal Aid Fund from public money. The Board's chairman is a layperson and the Board's members are chosen from people with knowledge of the legal system, and economic conditions. The Board's powers are contained in s 4 of the Act. It advises the Lord Chancellor on policy issues regarding legal services. They produce consultation papers (their recent proposals have been hotly debated). Section 5 of the Legal Aid Act 1988 sets out the duties of the Board which include reporting annually to the Lord Chancellor.

The legal aid scheme

The legal aid scheme has three main threads each having different rules and procedures.

Legal advice and assistance

If an individual is not sure whether he qualifies for legal aid he can take advantage of the £5 fixed fee interviews. A solicitor will advise him for a £5 fee. This is not subject to any means test, the service is available to everyone. The fixed fee interview only covers initial advice; the solicitor will not at this stage undertake any action on behalf of the client.

The Green Form scheme

The Green Form scheme was established by the Legal Advice and Assistance Act 1972 and is now embodied in Part III of the Legal Aid Act 1988. This scheme will cover practical assistance from the solicitor, he will advise, write letters, or negotiate for the client, he can consult a barrister regarding the client's case; it covers all legal services up to (but not including) representation in court. Representation in court is further provided for under the Green Form scheme if the client meets the necessary qualifying criteria. The Lord Chancellor can authorise free Green Form advice as under the duty solicitor scheme, and he has the power to eliminate certain areas from the scheme, such as wills and conveyancing. The Green Form scheme has been commended as useful and worthwhile, allowing people to have access to consult a solicitor. In their study 'The Operation of the Green Form scheme in England and Wales' (1988) *New Law Journal*, Baldwin and Hill praise the scheme noting that a great number of people used it and found it beneficial. This research is often put forward as a justification for retaining the Green Form scheme when critics advocate that the system is abused by many solicitors making inflated claims on Green Forms. Though Baldwin and Hill found no evidence to support this, they assert that instances of abuse of the scheme are rare.

Civil legal aid

Legal aid is available for proceedings at all civil courts and at some tribunals, for example, the employment appeal tribunal and the land tribunal. Legal aid is available to assist with the cost of all pre-court work and including representation in the court, Part V of the Legal Aid Act 1988 governs this area. Civil legal aid is demand led and the solicitor will determine whether he thinks the client will be able to meet the necessary criteria set.

Eligibility

Section 15(2) of the Legal Aid Act 1988 states that:

A person shall not be granted representation for the purposes of any proceedings unless he satisfies the board that he has reasonable grounds for taking, defending or being a party to the proceedings.

The party must satisfy the required financial eligibility criteria, which will determine whether the party has to pay a contribution towards the costs. The second requirement for eligibility is the 'merits of the case' test. This is the so-called reasonable test which has to be met in accordance with s 15(3) of the Legal Aid Act 1988. The party must satisfy the Board that they have reasonable grounds for bringing the action and for legal aid to be granted. The Board can refuse the application if, for example, the conduct of the party does not meet with the approval of the court, or the proceedings would not be cost effective. The Board has established certain standards which are applied to civil legal aid applications. The Local Legal Aid Office must assess the merits of the case and decide whether it has a reasonable chance of succeeding. The financial and reasonable test must both be satisfied. This second limb of the qualifying criteria is linked with the 'paying client' test; that is, where a party who is able to meet the cost of the litigation, proceed with the litigation after balancing the cost of the proceedings with the matter to be determined. If the applicant succeeds with his action then the property or money he recovers from the litigation may be subject to the statutory charge.

Legal aid does not exist to provide a free legal service. Legal aid is undergoing a lot of scrutiny and all avenues are being explored in a bid to reduce the escalating cost of the scheme. One idea being promoted is mediation, which commentators believe will reduce the legal aid bill. In his article 'Saving Costs and time with ADR' (1993) *Solicitors Journal* Andrew Thomas states that:

... evidence has emerged of a technique which helps to shorten disputes, saves costs and is successful in about 80% of cases, the technique is mediation.

He further goes on to say that:

Mediation appears to offer the prospect of considerable savings to the Legal Aid Board. However, the Board stated that legal aid is not available for alternative dispute resolution, because legal aid is only to be used in recognised court proceedings, and not in alternative methods.

It is argued that more use should be made of mediation and that it is a viable contender in the fight to reduce the soaring legal aid costs.

Criminal legal aid

Part V of the Legal Aid Act 1988 governs criminal proceedings in the magistrates' court, the Crown Court, the Court of Appeal and the House of Lords. The courts have the power to grant legal aid in criminal cases where this will be in the interests of justice. In criminal proceedings an application is made for legal aid to the magistrates, this will be decided by the magistrates' clerk. The legal aid will entail representation by a solicitor and preparation of the client's case.

Until 1982, in the Crown Courts, almost every defendant was granted legal aid. Sometimes a defendant will be asked to contribute to the costs, his financial circumstances will be taken into consideration and any person in receipt of income support will automatically qualify for legal aid. It is in the magistrates' courts that most people will find themselves unrepresented since the cases are of a less serious nature. The Legal Aid Act 1982 tried to address this balance and introduced a duty solicitor scheme in magistrates' courts. These 24 hour duty solicitors were seen as representing safeguards against the increase in police powers conferred by the Police and Criminal Evidence Act 1984. A further demand that is considered in the granting of legal aid whether the interests of justice will be served if the defendant is granted legal assistance. Section 22(2) of the Legal Aid Act 1982 sets out criteria which must be met to decide whether to grant legal aid. Section 22 of the Act states that legal aid should be granted if the offence is likely to result in 'a sentence which would deprive the accused of his likelihood or serious damage to his reputation'. Other criteria are if the accused is incapable of comprehending the proceedings because he cannot speak English, or has some form of mental or physical impairment, or if the case involves a point of law.

Criminal legal aid orders

Recent research by the Law Society has shown that there is an 8% overall reduction in the amount of criminal legal aid orders being granted by magistrates' courts between 1991 and 1992. This decrease in criminal legal aid orders can be attributed to a variety of factors. It is argued that some magistrates' courts are taking a very cautious approach to the granting of criminal legal aid orders if the defendant is not likely to be given a custodial sentence. This was reinforced by the Criminal Justice Act 1991, the aim of which, *inter alia,* was to divert as many offenders as possible away from custodial sentences and give community service instead. However, there seem to be fears growing amongst lawyers that many justices' clerks view community service as not falling within the ambit of the 1988 Act provisions. It is said by lawyers involved in criminal cases that judges have ruled that community service did not really involve any loss of liberty and therefore it did not meet the criteria set out in s 22 of the 1988 Act. 'A sentence which would deprive the accused of his liberty or lead to loss of his livelihood or serious damage to his reputation.' Another factor in the drop of criminal legal aid orders is the decrease in the number of cases coming before the courts. The police and the manner in which they deal with complaints have contributed to this. Resources tend to be targeted towards complaints which will have a strong chance of gaining a conviction. The changes in sentencing brought about by the Criminal Justice Act 1991 has seen an increase in the use of the 'caution' by police, and alternative methods of deterrent strategies. N Choen in 'Jails Empty as Crime Soars' ((1993) *Independent on Sunday)* found that in Wolverhampton there was a 17.8% reduction in prosecutions between 1991 and 1992 because of a 50.1% increase in the amount of cautions given by the police. Further, the Criminal Justice Act 1991 has substantially changed the way in which young offenders are dealt with in the Criminal Justice system. Section 68 together with Schedule 8 means more 17-year-olds are dealt with by the Youth Court and s 69 enables 16-year-olds to plead guilty to an offence by post. There is a determined effort to remove 14-year-olds out of the criminal justice system which reduces the number of juvenile cases. A further factor is that the Crown Prosecution Service is displaying a tendency to stop cases from continuing if they appear weak, to save costs.

Rights of appeal

An applicant who has his application turned down for legal aid can renew his application orally to the court or to the justice's clerk (reg 14 of the Legal Aid in Criminal and Care Proceedings (General) Regulations 1989). Regulation 15 provides that an application can be made for review to the relevant area committee of the Legal Aid Board. This procedure is not available for summary only offences or where the refusal of the application was for financial reasons. The application must be made within 14 days of the date of notification of the refusal.

Lord Chancellor's Advisory Committee on legal aid

Section 35 of the Legal Aid Act 1988 maintains the powers of this Committee. They report to the Lord Chancellor annually. However, the Legal Aid Board appears to overlap with the Advisory Committee and its continued existence is under review.

Standard fees

In 1993 standard fees for legal aid in magistrates' courts were introduced. This is to be extended to the Crown Courts. The lawyers remuneration is now based on an hourly rate, as opposed to the amount of work done. These proposals it is argued are an attack on the whole system of legal aid in criminal cases, and can only lead to lawyers practising in this area to consider a change. It is uncertain and fluctuating by nature, and because the increase in legal aid rates are well below the rate of inflation, it is no longer argued the profession to do the work profitably. In 1986 a joint study by the Law Society and the Lord Chancellor's Department demonstrated that it was only a minority of firms who were able to continue the work without making a loss. It is argued that in the last five years, expenses, which have been incurred by the practitioners, have increased 78.8%, however, the rates have only risen by 37.5% during the same period.

Grant rates for selected courts

(Fourth quarter 1992 over fourth quarter 1991)

MAGISTRATES' COURT	ORDERS GRANTED		% CHANGE
	1991	1992	
Cardiff	1930	1907	-1.19
Bridlington	131	110	-16.03
Southampton	802	776	-3.24
Hull	1237	1010	-18.35
Sunderland	784	667	-14.92
Swansea	920	933	1.41
Birmingham	2702	2043	-24.39
Nottingham	1879	1832	-2.50
Huddersfield	486	448	-7.82
S Western (London)	851	772	-9.28
S Bedfordshire	661	596	-9.83
Ipswich	502	469	-6.57
Harrogate	299	305	2.01
Leeds	2094	1865	-10.94
Sheffield	2021	2034	0.64
Barnsley	528	586	10.98
ALL COURTS TOTAL	17827	16353	-8.27

Law Society (1993) *Law Gazette*

Legal aid franchising

Many solicitors who rely on legal aid as a substantial part of their fee income are anxious about the Legal Aid Board's proposals in 'Franchising: the Next Steps'. Firms of solicitors who obtain a franchise will be considerably better off than those who do not, and the Legal Aid Board will, in time, transform into a controlling body monitoring the quality of franchised firms. In order for a firm of solicitors to apply for a franchise they have to comply with the Legal Aid Boards requirements. The underlying philosophy of the Board's proposals is that the legal process can be industrialised. The Legal Aid Board is insistent on specific criteria being met, and that 'systems' are firmly implemented;

the firms not being able to practice on an *ad hoc* basis. The Board emphasises the necessity for 'strategic management' and for firms who are seeking a franchise to have created a strategic plan for their business. This is to be a three to five year plan and include the geographical areas to be covered by the practice; the objective is to provide a quality legal advice service for clients. The Legal Aid Board have asserted that if firms wish to implement quality management systems specific standards must be met such as:

• strategic management;
• personnel management;
• service plan;
• case management;
• management of information; and
• financial information.

This may have consequences for small firms who may not have the resources to establish effective quality management systems. Meeting the quality criteria will be a requirement of every franchise; many members of the profession fear that, despite reassurance from the government, they will not be able to continue to provide legal aid services, unless they have a franchise.

Legal Aid Board's proposed systems

Personnel management

This will include an induction process and appraisal process, based on objective criteria for all staff. Staff who fail to meet the required standard will be given training and supervision until they reach the approved standard.

Case management

The firm must maintain written procedures for taking instructions case planning and closing. A plan for internal audits of case files must be implemented.

Service plan

This is a document which will contain, *inter alia*, a description of the legal aid services offered, how they are to be promoted, and how the client can gain access to the service.

Client care

Client care will be centred on Practice Rule 15. Other requirements will be appropriate language facilities and access to the disabled. A complaints system must record remedial action taken and its outcome. Existing and potential legal aid clients have to be given a copy of the leaflet used in the Birmingham Project, 'Legal Aid: A Quality Service' (1993) *Solicitors Journal*.

Many solicitors are already feeling the implications of fee-earning and standard fees; they assert the amount of administrative work they have to do has increased. Every applicant for criminal legal aid has now to produce documentary evidence to support their claim for legal aid eg a rent book, wage slips, income support books etc. The solicitor must ensure this evidence is available. If a client makes a false representation regarding their means to the solicitor the solicitor must report the client to the 'proper officer', ie the clerk to the justices in the magistrates' court. This is much the same as reg 67 of the Civil Legal Aid (General) Regulations. In civil legal aid it is difficult to give an exact account of financial eligibility. If a client disagrees the financial decisions there is no appeal against them. They can ask the Assessment Officer for a review. The case of *R v Legal Aid Assessment Office ex p Crocker* (1993) demonstrated that using assessments can be judicially reviewed and highlighted the gross unfairness of their being no appeal system in these cases.

Competitive tendering

Another concern that is facing solicitors regarding the Legal Aid Board's franchising ideas is that it will be a step towards competitive tendering for legal aid work. These firms which reached the minimum standard laid down by the Legal Aid Board would be invited to tender for legal aid work with the lowest bid getting the contract. These firms would handle blocks of legal aid work, which will restrict the right of an individual to choose his own solicitor. Lord Mackay has stated:

Firms offered a block contract will probably seek an assured volume of cases, and this may require some restriction on the number of firms offering legal aid. I can envisage that in some areas and for some types of work, only accredited firms which, given an assured standard of service, might be eligible to do legal aid cases.

((1993) *The Times*s, 22 January)

Legal aid for children

One of the main aims of the Children Act 1989 was that children with sufficient age and understanding should have their voices heard by the courts. This is embodied in s 1(3)(a) of the 1989 Act which states that 'the ascertainable wishes and feelings of the child concerned (considered in the light of his age and understanding)' must be taken into consideration; the welfare principle. Children now have greater rights of self-determination, this was made clear in the case of *Gillick v West Norfolk and Wisbech Area Health Authority* (1986). In this case a Department of Health and Social Security circular was distributed to doctors advising, *inter alia*, that they could, in certain circumstances, prescribe contraceptives to girls under the age of 16 without parental consent. Mrs Gillick bought an action against the DHSS and her local authority hospital. The case went to the House of Lords. It was a landmark decision in children's rights as it recognised that children, particularly those of a certain age and understanding should have a greater say in decisions concerning them. Rule 9.2A(1) of the Family Proceedings Rules 1991 recognises this principle. Children are now entitled to make their own applications to court in family proceedings. Since 1989 a child legal aid eligibility has been based solely upon means; children complete a simplified statements of means (form CLA 4.F). The Legal Aid Board sends the form for assessment, even though the child declares he has no means. The merits of the case are considered with regard to s 15 of the Legal Aid Act 1988. However, evidence has suggested that it is increasingly the case that the Legal Aid Board is refusing legal aid for children to take proceedings, particularly if children wish to join in their parents' proceedings (*Re S (a Minor) (Independent Representation)* (1993)).

Criticisms of the legal aid scheme

In late 1990 the Lord Chancellor expressed his continuing concern over the spiralling cost of the legal aid system. He highlighted the £715 million cost of running the system which had doubled in the last five years. He declared that the legal aid fund was not a 'blank cheque' and that deep cuts would have to be made in the legal aid system.

Lord Mackay claimed that 'unless the legal aid system changes it will collapse under the weight of its ever increasing cost'.

Both LAG and the Law Society were scornful of the chancellor's remarks. They claimed that the increase in the cost of the legal aid system was a consequence of government policy and social trends, such as a rising crime rate. Lawyers were indignant and declared that they were not making high profits from the increase. The cuts will affect between 12 and 14 million people and will hit 37% of households. Lord Mackay defends his measures. He states that the costs of legal services are very high and are rising at such a rate that it is impossible to sustain such a rapid rate of growth. Lord Mackay has pointed out that he has looked at other possibilities to cut legal aid spending, for example, he looked at the scope of the service and whether it would be possible to remove legal aid from a particular area of work, but did not see this as a viable option (although in 1991 he did withdraw Green Form legal aid from refugees wanting asylum).

Unmet legal need

It is argued that vast areas of law, some with considerable importance in respect of individual rights, still remain uncovered by the legal aid scheme. As the criteria for legal aid eligibility become even more difficult, this can only get worse. Justice, it is said, in practice, will be available only to the very poor and the rich. Research has proved that in real terms lawyers are used only by a small social group in society, and only for a small proportion of specific areas. Many individuals who would benefit from the services of a lawyer do not take advantage of the service. A variety of reasons have been articulated for this, mostly concerning the fact that lawyers are perceived as being very expensive and they might not be able to afford his fees; lawyers are also perceived as being unapproachable; they tend not to market themselves very well so that people might not believe that their problem is one that a lawyer could deal with.

Michael Zander in his study 'Who goes to Solicitors?' (1969) *Law Society's Gazette* pointed out that research studies have proved that people in the middle band of income range tended to use lawyers more (often for property matters) and that people of modest means were denied access to pursue a legitimate claim because of this 'middle income trap'.

The public, it is said, have a very restricted view of the type of work a lawyer can undertake which leads to many problems being unresolved which could be solved by legal means. The profession itself have taken a very narrow view of the type of work that lawyers will undertake. This can be attributed to the actual training of lawyers where emphasis is laid on more profitable subject areas such as commercial and company law; subject areas like landlord and tenant and welfare law remaining merely options to young would be lawyers. This still remains the case even though the Marre Report, 'A Time for Change', 1988, recommended more involvement of lawyers in areas such as immigration and housing. The Marre Report also recommended that lawyers must promote more public education and awareness of the legal profession; they should attempt to be more approachable to help reduce public fear of lawyers, particularly in respect of ethnic minority groups who often feel intimidated by the profession.

Reform

In 1996 a White Paper proposing further legislation in respect of legal aid was published entitled 'Striking the Balance: The Future of Legal Aid in England and Wales' (Cmnd 3305). Some changes will have delayed implementation because of difficulties derived from the government's decision not to introduce a Legal Aid Bill in the Parliamentary session 1996–97.

Main proposals of the White Paper

Cash limits in the form of pre-determined budgets to curb 'demand led' legal aid. From 1996–97 the legal aid bill rose by 10% prompting Lord McKay to comment it could no longer go on. Serious cases, such as fraud, will be allocated separate budgets. A new 'merits' test for civil legal aid will be introduced to ensure that deserving cases are heard. Criminal legal aid will still be awarded in line with the 'interest of justice' criterion. All recipients of legal aid should make some form of contribution to the legal aid scheme and possible liability for the opponents costs could be incurred. The Legal Aid Board will be able to recover costs from the future sale of a house. It has been possible since 1996 to take into account the market value of an applicant's house not previously included in the calculations. Wider provision of legal services are to be offered by a variety of agencies which will be quality controlled and have set budgets (Example CAE3). The Legal Aid Board will award block contracts with fixed prices. Alternative dispute resolution will be strongly favoured to alleviate the burden on the legal aid budget.

Critics of the proposals argue it will cause extreme hardship to poorer litigants and widen the already vast track of litigants cut off from the court system with no access to justice.

Trade unions

These offer invaluable help and advice to their members in employment matters. They can mediate between a party and an employer and represent their members at industrial tribunals.

Alternative legal services

There exists a wide range of alternative sources outside the legal system offering low cost legal advice. The Lord Chancellor, in his bid to reduce the legal aid bill is firmly behind the procedures of mediation, conciliation and arbitration.

Mediation

If both parties consent a mediator can be used to reach a settlement in a dispute.

Mediation does not debar the parties from the court system, if one party does not agree with the decision they can seek further redress from the courts.

Conciliation

Like mediation an independent mediator will act as an arbitrator between the parties to find an acceptable solution to the dispute.

Arbitration

In this system an arbitrator, usually agreed on by the parties, hears the evidence from both sides and tries to settle the dispute amicably. It is slightly more formal than mediation in that the arbitrator's decision can be binding on the parties and can debar them from further redress through the courts. Business contracts usually contain an arbitration clause which stipulates any disputes must go through this system before any application to the normal courts.

Law centres

The establishment of these centres was made in 1968 by the Society of Labour Lawyers in 'Justice for All'. They were intended to provide a legal service outside normal office hours; help educate the public in their rights and duties under the law and specialise in specific areas of law which were seen as appropriate to poorer sections of the community such as landlord and tenant, employment law and social security law. However, the law centres are declining in number and they are fighting a battle to obtain funds to allow them to go on providing their free service. Increased government funding is necessary if law centres are to continue helping to meet a part of the unmet legal need.

Duty solicitor's schemes

Duty solicitor's schemes are based locally and organised by the Law Society. The first scheme was established in 1972. Volunteer solicitors attend magistrates' courts according to a rota and interview defendants in custody who are not legally represented.

The stringent cuts being made in the legal aid eligibility will have the effect of disenfranchising a vast amount of individuals from the justice system. Justice will be the preserve of the rich or the very badly off, those in middle incomes will be unable to afford litigation no matter how legitimate this claim may be.

Citizen's Advice Bureaux

These are run by charitable organisations. They have a network of offices throughout the UK, normally staffed by trained volunteers. They will assist in writing letters and mediating between the parties, they also represent clients in the lower courts.

Regulators

Disputes which involve problems with large industries in the public and private sector are best settled through this system. A regulator is set up by the particular industry, they will investigate the complaint and try to find an amicable solution.

Ombudsman

First set up by the banking industry, the ombudsman plays an important role in settling disputes in particular industries and professions. Usually the individual must go through all the internal complaints procedures in a particular industry/profession before consulting the ombudsman. The parties are not debarred from taking their dispute through the normal courts if not satisfied with the outcome.

Index